Entertainment Directory

PITTSBURGH RESTAURANT GUIDE 2018

RESTAURANTS, BARS & CAFES

★★★★★

The Most Positively Reviewed and Recommended Restaurants in the City

EGP *Editorial*

PITTSBURGH RESTAURANT GUIDE 2018
Best Rated Restaurants in Pittsburgh, Pennsylvania

© Arthur S. Emerson, 2018
© E.G.P. Editorial, 2018

Printed in USA.

ISBN-13: 978-1545208359
ISBN-10: 1545208352

Copyright © 2018
All rights reserved.

PITTSBURGH RESTAURANTS 2018
The Most Recommended Restaurants in Pittsburgh

This directory is dedicated to the Business Owners and Managers who provide the experience that the locals and tourists enjoy. Thanks you very much for all that you do and thank for being the "People Choice".

Thanks to everyone that posts their reviews online and the amazing reviews sites that make our life easier.

The places listed in this book are the most positively reviewed and recommended by locals and travelers from around the world.

Thank you for your time and enjoy the directory that is designed with locals and tourist in mind!

TOP 500 RESTAURANTS
Ranked from #1 to #500

Pittsburgh Restaurant Guide 2018 / Restaurants, Bars & Cafés

#1
Gaucho Parrilla Argentina
Cuisines: Argentine
Average price: Modest
Area: Strip District
Address: 1601 Penn Ave
Pittsburgh, PA 15222
Phone: (412) 709-6622

#2
täkō
Cuisines: American, Mexican
Average price: Modest
Area: Downtown
Address: 214 6th St
Pittsburgh, PA 15222
Phone: (412) 471-8256

#3
Las Palmas
Cuisines: Mexican
Average price: Inexpensive
Area: Oakland
Address: 326 Atwood St
Pittsburgh, PA 15213
Phone: (412) 682-1115

#4
Altius
Cuisines: American
Average price: Expensive
Area: Duquesne Heights
Address: 1230 Grandview Ave
Pittsburgh, PA 15211
Phone: (412) 904-4442

#5
Butcher and the Rye
Cuisines: American
Average price: Expensive
Area: Downtown
Address: 212 6th St
Pittsburgh, PA 15222
Phone: (412) 391-2752

#6
Cop Out Pierogies
Cuisines: Polish, American
Average price: Inexpensive
Area: Etna
Address: 350 Butler St
Pittsburgh, PA 15223
Phone: (412) 973-0068

#7
Umbrella Cafe
Cuisines: Cafe, Bakery, Juice Bar
Average price: Inexpensive
Area: Downtown
Address: 951 Liberty Ave
Pittsburgh, PA 15222
Phone: (412) 391-8500

#8
Legume
Cuisines: French, American, Soul Food
Average price: Expensive
Area: Oakland
Address: 214 N Craig St
Pittsburgh, PA 15213
Phone: (412) 621-2700

#9
The Twisted Frenchman
Cuisines: French
Average price: Expensive
Area: East Liberty
Address: 128 S Highland Ave
Pittsburgh, PA 15206
Phone: (412) 361-1340

#10
Smallman Galley
Cuisines: American, Bar
Average price: Modest
Area: Strip District
Address: 54 21st St
Pittsburgh, PA 15222
Phone: (412) 904-2444

#11
Eleven
Cuisines: American
Average price: Expensive
Area: Strip District
Address: 1150 Smallman St
Pittsburgh, PA 15222
Phone: (412) 201-5656

#12
Doce Taqueria
Cuisines: Mexican
Average price: Inexpensive
Area: South Side
Address: 1220 E Carson St
Pittsburgh, PA 15203
Phone: (412) 238-8518

#13
Meat & Potatoes
Cuisines: Gastropub
Average price: Expensive
Area: Downtown
Address: 649 Penn Ave
Pittsburgh, PA 15222
Phone: (412) 325-7007

#14
Penn Ave Fish Company
Cuisines: Sushi Bar, Seafood, Seafood Market
Average price: Modest
Area: Strip District
Address: 2208 Penn Ave
Pittsburgh, PA 15222
Phone: (412) 434-7200

#15
Cafe' 33
Cuisines: Taiwanese
Average price: Modest
Area: Squirrel Hill
Address: 1711 Shady Ave
Pittsburgh, PA 15217
Phone: (412) 421-2717

#16
Cure
Cuisines: American, Mediterranean
Average price: Expensive
Area: Lawrenceville
Address: 5336 Butler St
Pittsburgh, PA 15201
Phone: (412) 252-2595

#17
Point Brugge Café
Cuisines: Belgian
Average price: Modest
Area: Point Breeze
Address: 401 Hastings St
Pittsburgh, PA 15206
Phone: (412) 441-3334

#18
Las Palmas Carniceria
Cuisines: Mexican
Average price: Inexpensive
Area: Brookline
Address: 700 Brookline Blvd
Pittsburgh, PA 15226
Phone: (412) 344-1131

#19
Bakersfield Penn Ave
Cuisines: Bar, Mexican
Average price: Modest
Area: Downtown
Address: 940 Penn Ave
Pittsburgh, PA 15222
Phone: (412) 586-5024

#20
Proper Brick Oven & Tap Room
Cuisines: Italian, Pizza, Bar
Average price: Modest
Area: Downtown
Address: 139 7th St
Pittsburgh, PA 15222
Phone: (412) 281-5700

#21
Alla Famiglia
Cuisines: Italian
Average price: Exclusive
Area: Allentown
Address: 804 E Warrington Ave
Pittsburgh, PA 15210
Phone: (412) 488-1440

#22
Peppi's
Cuisines: Sandwiches
Average price: Inexpensive
Area: North Side
Address: 927 Western Ave
Pittsburgh, PA 15233
Phone: (412) 231-9009

#23
Morcilla
Cuisines: Spanish
Average price: Expensive
Area: Lawrenceville
Address: 3519 Butler St
Pittsburgh, PA 15201
Phone: (412) 652-9924

#24
Cafe Du Jour
Cuisines: French
Average price: Modest
Area: South Side
Address: 1107 E Carson St
Pittsburgh, PA 15203
Phone: (412) 488-9695

Pittsburgh Restaurant Guide 2018 / Restaurants, Bars & Cafés

#25
The Pub Chip Shop
Cuisines: Bakery, Fish & Chips
Average price: Inexpensive
Area: South Side
Address: 1830 E Carson St
Pittsburgh, PA 15203
Phone: (412) 381-2447

#26
Butterjoint
Cuisines: American, Bar
Average price: Modest
Area: Oakland
Address: 214 N Craig St
Pittsburgh, PA 15213
Phone: (412) 621-2700

#27
Amazing Cafe
Cuisines: Cafe, Vegan, Gluten-Free
Average price: Modest
Area: South Side
Address: 1506 E Carson St
Pittsburgh, PA 15203
Phone: (412) 432-5950

#28
Fat Heads Saloon
Cuisines: American
Average price: Modest
Area: South Side
Address: 1805 E Carson St
Pittsburgh, PA 15203
Phone: (412) 431-7433

#29
Istanbul Sofra
Cuisines: Turkish, Mediterranean
Average price: Modest
Area: Regent Square
Address: 7600 Forbes Ave
Pittsburgh, PA 15221
Phone: (412) 727-6693

#30
La Palapa, Mexican Gourmet Kitchen
Cuisines: Mexican
Average price: Modest
Area: South Side
Address: 1925 E Carson St
Pittsburgh, PA 15203
Phone: (412) 586-7015

#31
Nicky's Thai Kitchen
Cuisines: Thai, Seafood, Vegan
Average price: Modest
Area: Downtown
Address: 903 Penn Ave
Pittsburgh, PA 15222
Phone: (412) 471-8424

#33
Tan Izakaya
Cuisines: Sushi Bar, Ramen
Average price: Modest
Area: Shadyside
Address: 815 S Aiken Ave
Pittsburgh, PA 15232
Phone: (412) 688-0188

#32
Edgar Tacos Stand
Cuisines: Street Vendor, Mexican
Average price: Inexpensive
Area: Strip District
Address: 2627 Penn Ave
Pittsburgh, PA 15222
Phone: (412) 849-8864

#34
Kaya
Cuisines: Caribbean, Bar
Average price: Modest
Area: Strip District
Address: 2000 Smallman St
Pittsburgh, PA 15222
Phone: (412) 261-6565

#35
The Smiling Moose
Cuisines: Bar, Music Venue, American
Average price: Modest
Area: South Side
Address: 1306 E Carson St
Pittsburgh, PA 15203
Phone: (412) 431-4668

#36
Park Bruges
Cuisines: Belgian
Average price: Modest
Area: Highland Park
Address: 5801 Bryant St
Pittsburgh, PA 15206
Phone: (412) 661-3334

#37
Monterey Bay Fish Grotto
Cuisines: Seafood
Average price: Expensive
Area: Duquesne Heights
Address: 1411 Grandview Ave
Pittsburgh, PA 15211
Phone: (412) 481-4414

#38
Burgatory
Cuisines: Burgers
Average price: Modest
Area: North Side
Address: 342 N Shore Dr
Pittsburgh, PA 15212
Phone: (412) 586-5846

#39
Winghart's Burger & Whiskey Bar
Cuisines: Burgers, Pizza, Whiskey Bar
Average price: Modest
Area: Downtown
Address: 5 Market Sq
Pittsburgh, PA 15222
Phone: (412) 434-5600

#40
Station
Cuisines: Cocktail Bar, American, Gastropub
Average price: Modest
Area: Bloomfield
Address: 4744 Liberty Ave
Pittsburgh, PA 15224
Phone: (412) 251-0540

#41
Streets On Carson
Cuisines: French, Bar
Average price: Inexpensive
Area: South Side
Address: 1120 E Carson st
Pittsburgh, PA 15203
Phone: (412) 918-1006

#42
Roasted Barrelhouse & Eatery
Cuisines: Cocktail Bar, Beer Bar, American
Average price: Modest
Area: Lawrenceville
Address: 3705 Butler St
Pittsburgh, PA 15201
Phone: (412) 904-3470

#43
Smiling Banana Leaf
Cuisines: Thai
Average price: Modest
Area: Highland Park
Address: 5901 Bryant St
Pittsburgh, PA 15206
Phone: (412) 362-3200

#44
Muddy Waters Oyster Bar
Cuisines: Cajun/Creole, Seafood
Average price: Modest
Area: East Liberty
Address: 130 S Highland Ave
Pittsburgh, PA 15206
Phone: (412) 361-0555

#45
Alihan's Mediterranean Cuisine
Cuisines: Mediterranean, Turkish
Average price: Modest
Area: Downtown
Address: 124 6th St
Pittsburgh, PA 15222
Phone: (412) 888-0630

#46
Piccolo Forno
Cuisines: Italian, Pizza
Average price: Modest
Area: Lawrenceville
Address: 3801 Butler St
Pittsburgh, PA 15201
Phone: (412) 622-0111

#47
YinzBurgh BBQ
Cuisines: Barbeque, Southern, Vegan
Average price: Modest
Area: Bloomfield
Address: 4903 Baum Blvd
Pittsburgh, PA 15213
Phone: (412) 621-9469

#48
Pasha Cafe Lounge
Cuisines: Mediterranean,
Turkish, Breakfast & Brunch
Average price: Modest
Area: Shadyside
Address: 808 Ivy Street
Pittsburgh, PA 15232
Phone: (412) 688-7415

#49
Sienna Mercato
Cuisines: Italian, Pizza, Cocktail Bar
Average price: Modest
Area: Downtown
Address: 942 Penn Ave
Pittsburgh, PA 15222
Phone: (412) 281-2810

#50
Everyday Noodles
Cuisines: Chinese, Noodles
Average price: Modest
Area: Squirrel Hill
Address: 5875 Forbes Ave
Pittsburgh, PA 15217
Phone: (412) 421-6668

#51
Twelve Whiskey Barbecue
Cuisines: Barbeque
Average price: Modest
Area: South Side
Address: 1222 East Carson St
Pittsburgh, PA 15203
Phone: (412) 742-4024

#52
Dish Osteria and Bar
Cuisines: Italian
Average price: Expensive
Area: South Side
Address: 128 S 17th St
Pittsburgh, PA 15203
Phone: (412) 390-2012

#53
The Dor-Stop Restaurant
Cuisines: Breakfast & Brunch, Diner
Average price: Inexpensive
Area: Dormont
Address: 1430 Potomac Ave
Pittsburgh, PA 15216
Phone: (412) 561-9320

#54
Hog's Head Bar & Grill
Cuisines: American, Bar, Pizza
Average price: Modest
Area: West View
Address: 3433 Spring Garden Rd
Pittsburgh, PA 15212
Phone: (412) 251-0439

#55
Family Restaurant
Cuisines: Middle Eastern, Greek, American
Average price: Modest
Area: Carrick
Address: 2614 Brownsville Rd
Pittsburgh, PA 15227
Phone: (412) 881-8550

#56
Kaleidoscope Café
Cuisines: American, Cafe
Average price: Modest
Area: Lawrenceville
Address: 108 43rd St
Pittsburgh, PA 15201
Phone: (412) 683-4004

#57
Seviche
Cuisines: Cuban, Latin American, Tapas/Small Plates
Average price: Modest
Area: Downtown
Address: 930 Penn Ave
Pittsburgh, PA 15222
Phone: (412) 697-3120

#58
Bigham Tavern
Cuisines: Chicken Wings, Pub, Breakfast & Brunch
Average price: Modest
Area: Mt. Washington
Address: 321 Bigham St
Pittsburgh, PA 15211
Phone: (412) 431-9313

#59
Subba
Cuisines: Asian Fusion
Average price: Inexpensive
Area: North Side
Address: 700 Cedar Ave
Pittsburgh, PA 15212
Phone: (412) 586-5764

#60
Pear and the Pickle, Cafe & Market
Cuisines: Cafe, Fruits & Veggies, Grocery
Average price: Inexpensive
Area: Troy Hill
Address: 1800 Rialto St
Pittsburgh, PA 15212
Phone: (412) 322-0333

#61
Deluca's Diner
Cuisines: Breakfast & Brunch
Average price: Inexpensive
Area: Strip District
Address: 2015 Penn Ave
Pittsburgh, PA 15222
Phone: (412) 566-2195

#62
Big Shot Bob's House of Wings
Cuisines: Chicken Wings, Burgers, Sandwiches
Average price: Inexpensive
Area: Avalon
Address: 344 Union Ave
Pittsburgh, PA 15202
Phone: (412) 761-7468

#63
Applewood Smoke Burger Company
Cuisines: Burgers, Vegetarian, Sandwiches
Average price: Modest
Area: Highland Park
Address: 5721 Bryant St
Pittsburgh, PA 15206
Phone: (412) 522-4592

#64
Spice Island Tea House
Cuisines: Asian Fusion, Tea Room, Thai
Average price: Modest
Area: Oakland
Address: 253 Atwood St
Pittsburgh, PA 15213
Phone: (412) 687-8821

#65
Bar Marco
Cuisines: Wine Bar, Cafe
Average price: Modest
Area: Strip District
Address: 2216 Penn Ave
Pittsburgh, PA 15222
Phone: (412) 471-1900

#66
Pusadee's Garden
Cuisines: Thai
Average price: Modest
Area: Lawrenceville
Address: 5321 Butler St
Pittsburgh, PA 15201
Phone: (412) 781-8724

#67
Showcase BBQ
Cuisines: Barbeque
Average price: Inexpensive
Area: Homewood
Address: 6800 Frankstown Ave
Pittsburgh, PA 15208
Phone: (412) 361-7469

#68
Spoon
Cuisines: American
Average price: Expensive
Area: Shadyside
Address: 134 S Highland Ave
Pittsburgh, PA 15206
Phone: (412) 362-6001

#69
Hofbrauhaus Pittsburgh
Cuisines: German, Pub
Average price: Modest
Area: South Side
Address: 2705 S Water St
Pittsburgh, PA 15203
Phone: (412) 224-2328

#70
Turkish Kebab House
Cuisines: Turkish
Average price: Modest
Area: Squirrel Hill
Address: 5819 Forbes Ave
Pittsburgh, PA 15217
Phone: (412) 422-4100

#71
Luke Wholey's Wild Alaskan Grille
Cuisines: Seafood, Sushi Bar, Cocktail Bar
Average price: Modest
Area: Strip District
Address: 2106 Penn Ave
Pittsburgh, PA 15222
Phone: (412) 904-4509

#72
G & G Noodle Bar
Cuisines: Noodles
Average price: Modest
Area: Downtown
Address: 535 Liberty Ave
Pittsburgh, PA 15222
Phone: (412) 281-4748

#73
The Vandal
Cuisines: Sandwiches, Cafe
Average price: Modest
Area: Lawrenceville
Address: 4306 Butler St
Pittsburgh, PA 15201
Phone: (412) 251-0465

#74
Teppanyaki Kyoto
Cuisines: Japanese
Average price: Modest
Area: Highland Park
Address: 5808 Bryant St
Pittsburgh, PA 15206
Phone: (412) 441-1610

#75
Sichuan Gourmet
Cuisines: Szechuan
Average price: Modest
Area: Oakland
Address: 328 Atwood St
Pittsburgh, PA 15213
Phone: (412) 621-6889

#76
The Summit
Cuisines: Cocktail Bar, American
Average price: Modest
Area: Mt. Washington
Address: 200 Shiloh St
Pittsburgh, PA 15211
Phone: (412) 918-1647

#77
Tessaro's
Cuisines: Steakhouse, Burgers, American
Average price: Modest
Area: Bloomfield
Address: 4601 Liberty Ave
Pittsburgh, PA 15224
Phone: (412) 682-6809

#78
Nadine's
Cuisines: American, Diner
Average price: Inexpensive
Area: South Side
Address: 19 S 27th St
Pittsburgh, PA 15203
Phone: (412) 481-1793

#79
Carmi Family Restaurant
Cuisines: Soul Food
Average price: Modest
Area: North Side
Address: 917 Western Ave
Pittsburgh, PA 15233
Phone: (412) 231-0100

#80
Nicky's Thai Kitchen
Cuisines: Thai
Average price: Modest
Area: North Side
Address: 856 Western Ave
Pittsburgh, PA 15233
Phone: (412) 321-8424

#81
The Urban Tap
Cuisines: Gastropub
Average price: Modest
Area: South Side
Address: 1209 E Carson St
Pittsburgh, PA 15203
Phone: (412) 586-7499

#82
Piper's Pub
Cuisines: British, Irish, Pub
Average price: Modest
Area: South Side
Address: 1828 E Carson St
Pittsburgh, PA 15203
Phone: (412) 381-3977

#83
Spork
Cuisines: Tapas/Small Plates, Italian, Cocktail Bar
Average price: Expensive
Area: Bloomfield
Address: 5430 Penn Ave
Pittsburgh, PA 15206
Phone: (412) 441-1700

#84
Sesame Garden
Cuisines: Chinese
Average price: Modest
Area: Mt. Washington
Address: 202 Shiloh St
Pittsburgh, PA 15211
Phone: (412) 481-8282

#85
Shiloh Grill
Cuisines: Pub, American, Gastropub
Average price: Modest
Area: Mt. Washington
Address: 123 Shiloh St
Pittsburgh, PA 15211
Phone: (412) 431-4000

#86
The Greek Gourmet
Cuisines: Greek
Average price: Inexpensive
Area: Squirrel Hill
Address: 2130 Murray Ave
Pittsburgh, PA 15217
Phone: (412) 422-2998

#87
Tram's Kitchen
Cuisines: Vietnamese
Average price: Inexpensive
Area: Bloomfield
Address: 4050 Penn Ave
Pittsburgh, PA 15224
Phone: (412) 682-2688

#88
Kevin's Deli
Cuisines: Deli
Average price: Inexpensive
Area: Oakland
Address: 101 N Dithridge St
Pittsburgh, PA 15213
Phone: (412) 621-6368

#89
Carmella's Plates & Pints
Cuisines: Cocktail Bar, American
Average price: Modest
Area: South Side
Address: 1908 E Carson St
Pittsburgh, PA 15203
Phone: (412) 918-1215

#90
Kavsar Restaurant
Cuisines: Halal, Uzbek, Russian
Average price: Modest
Area: Mt. Washington
Address: 16 Southern Ave
Pittsburgh, PA 15211
Phone: (412) 488-8708

#91
Madonna's Mediterranean Cuisine
Cuisines: Mediterranean
Average price: Inexpensive
Area: Downtown
Address: 408 Smithfield St
Pittsburgh, PA 15219
Phone: (412) 281-4693

#92
Hough's
Cuisines: Sports Bar, American
Average price: Modest
Area: Greenfield
Address: 563 Greenfield Ave
Pittsburgh, PA 15207
Phone: (412) 586-5944

#93
El Burro
Cuisines: Mexican
Average price: Inexpensive
Area: North Side
Address: 1108 Federal St
Pittsburgh, PA 15212
Phone: (412) 904-3451

#94
Sienna On The Square
Cuisines: Italian, Wine Bar
Average price: Modest
Area: Downtown
Address: 22 Market Sq
Pittsburgh, PA 15222
Phone: (412) 281-6363

#95
Michael's Pizza Bar & Restaurant
Cuisines: Pizza
Average price: Inexpensive
Area: South Side
Address: 2612 Sarah St
Pittsburgh, PA 15203
Phone: (412) 381-6102

#96
Big Jim's Restaurant & Bar
Cuisines: American, Italian
Average price: Modest
Area: Greenfield
Address: 201 Saline St
Pittsburgh, PA 15207
Phone: (412) 421-0532

#97
Cambod-Ican Kitchen
Cuisines: Cambodian, Asian Fusion, Seafood
Average price: Modest
Area: South Side
Address: 1701 E Carson St
Pittsburgh, PA 15203
Phone: (412) 381-6199

#98
Grandma B's
Cuisines: Halal, Diner, Breakfast & Brunch
Average price: Inexpensive
Area: The Hill District
Address: 2537 Wylie Ave
Pittsburgh, PA 15219
Phone: (412) 681-4087

#99
Smoke BBQ Taqueria
Cuisines: Barbeque
Average price: Modest
Area: Lawrenceville
Address: 4115 Butler St
Pittsburgh, PA 15201
Phone: (412) 224-2070

#100
Tamarind
Cuisines: Indian
Average price: Modest
Area: Oakland
Address: 257 N Craig St
Pittsburgh, PA 15213
Phone: (412) 605-0500

#101
Legends of The North Shore
Cuisines: Italian
Average price: Modest
Area: North Side
Address: 500 E N Ave
Pittsburgh, PA 15212
Phone: (412) 321-8000

#102
Micro Diner
Cuisines: Diner, Breakfast & Brunch
Average price: Inexpensive
Area: Mt. Washington
Address: 221 Shiloh St
Pittsburgh, PA 15211
Phone: (412) 381-1391

#103
Cafe Zinho
Cuisines: Portuguese, Mediterranean
Average price: Modest
Area: Shadyside
Address: 238 Spahr St
Pittsburgh, PA 15232
Phone: (412) 363-1500

#104
Bluebird Kitchen
Cuisines: American, Breakfast & Brunch
Average price: Modest
Area: Downtown
Address: 221 Forbes Ave
Pittsburgh, PA 15222
Phone: (412) 642-4414

#105
Max's Allegheny Tavern
Cuisines: German, Pub
Average price: Modest
Area: North Side
Address: 537 Suismon St
Pittsburgh, PA 15212
Phone: (412) 231-1899

#106
The Commoner
Cuisines: American, Cocktail Bar
Average price: Modest
Area: Downtown
Address: 458 Strawberry Way
Pittsburgh, PA 15219
Phone: (412) 230-4800

#107
Red Oak Cafe
Cuisines: Deli, Sandwiches, American
Average price: Inexpensive
Area: Oakland
Address: 3610 Forbes Ave
Pittsburgh, PA 15213
Phone: (412) 621-2221

#108
Conicella Pizza
Cuisines: Pizza
Average price: Inexpensive
Area: Greenfield
Address: 422 Greenfield Ave
Pittsburgh, PA 15207
Phone: (412) 521-6570

#109
Pastitsio
Cuisines: Greek, Mediterranean, Street Vendor
Average price: Modest
Area: Lawrenceville
Address: 3716 Butler St
Pittsburgh, PA 15201
Phone: (412) 586-7656

#110
Eden
Cuisines: Vegan, Live/Raw Food
Average price: Modest
Area: Shadyside
Address: 735 Copeland St
Pittsburgh, PA 15232
Phone: (412) 802-7070

#111
Brillobox
Cuisines: Bar, Music Venue, Vegetarian
Average price: Modest
Area: Bloomfield
Address: 4104 Penn Ave
Pittsburgh, PA 15224
Phone: (412) 621-4900

#112
Union Grill
Cuisines: American
Average price: Modest
Area: Oakland
Address: 413 S Craig St
Pittsburgh, PA 15213
Phone: (412) 681-8620

#113
Tan Lac Vien
Cuisines: Vietnamese, Vegetarian
Average price: Modest
Area: Squirrel Hill
Address: 2114 Murray Ave
Pittsburgh, PA 15217
Phone: (412) 521-8888

#114
NOLA
Cuisines: Cajun/Creole
Average price: Modest
Area: Downtown
Address: 24 Market Sq
Pittsburgh, PA 15222
Phone: (412) 471-9100

#115
Church Brew Works
Cuisines: Bar, American
Average price: Modest
Area: Lawrenceville
Address: 3525 Liberty Ave
Pittsburgh, PA 15201
Phone: (412) 688-8200

#116
Sam's Sun Sandwich
Cuisines: Sandwiches, Mediterranean
Average price: Inexpensive
Area: Carrick
Address: 2616 Brownsville Rd
Pittsburgh, PA 15227
Phone: (412) 884-8120

#117
Crepes Parisiennes
Cuisines: Creperie, Desserts
Average price: Modest
Area: Oakland
Address: 207 S Craig St
Pittsburgh, PA 15213
Phone: (412) 683-1912

#118
Daphne Cafe
Cuisines: Mediterranean, Turkish
Average price: Modest
Area: Shadyside
Address: 5811 Ellsworth Ave
Pittsburgh, PA 15232
Phone: (412) 441-1130

#119
Sichuan Gourmet
Cuisines: Szechuan
Average price: Modest
Area: Squirrel Hill
Address: 1900 Murray Ave
Pittsburgh, PA 15217
Phone: (412) 521-1313

#120
Umami
Cuisines: Sushi Bar, Japanese, Bar
Average price: Modest
Area: Lawrenceville
Address: 202 38th St
Pittsburgh, PA 15201
Phone: (412) 224-2354

#121
Tender Bar & Kitchen
Cuisines: American, Cocktail Bar
Average price: Modest
Area: Lawrenceville
Address: 4300 Butler St
Pittsburgh, PA 15201
Phone: (412) 402-9522

#122
The Porch at Schenley
Cuisines: Sandwiches, American, Burgers
Average price: Modest
Area: Oakland
Address: 221 Schenley Dr
Pittsburgh, PA 15213
Phone: (412) 687-6724

#123
Stone Neapolitan Pizzeria
Cuisines: Pizza
Average price: Modest
Area: Downtown
Address: 300 Liberty Ave
Pittsburgh, PA 15222
Phone: (412) 904-4531

#124
Lola Bistro
Cuisines: American
Average price: Modest
Area: North Side
Address: 1100 Galveston Ave
Pittsburgh, PA 15233
Phone: (412) 322-1106

#125
Primanti Bros.
Cuisines: Sandwiches, American, Sports Bar
Average price: Inexpensive
Area: Strip District
Address: 46 18th St
Pittsburgh, PA 15222
Phone: (412) 263-2142

#126
Apsara Cafe
Cuisines: Thai, Cafe
Average price: Modest
Area: South Side
Address: 1703 E Carson St
Pittsburgh, PA 15203
Phone: (412) 251-0664

#127
Stagioni
Cuisines: Italian, Breakfast & Brunch
Average price: Modest
Area: South Side
Address: 2104 E Carson St
Pittsburgh, PA 15203
Phone: (412) 586-4738

#128
Allegheny Sandwich Shoppe
Cuisines: Breakfast & Brunch, Sandwiches
Average price: Inexpensive
Area: North Side
Address: 822 Western Ave
Pittsburgh, PA 15233
Phone: (412) 322-4797

#129
Fuel & Fuddle
Cuisines: Gastropub
Average price: Modest
Area: Oakland
Address: 212 Oakland Ave
Pittsburgh, PA 15213
Phone: (412) 682-3473

#130
Penn Avenue Fish Company
Cuisines: Sushi Bar, Seafood
Average price: Modest
Area: Downtown
Address: 308 Forbes Ave
Pittsburgh, PA 15222
Phone: (412) 562-1710

#131
El Milagro
Cuisines: Mexican
Average price: Modest
Area: Beechview
Address: 1542 Beechview Ave
Pittsburgh, PA 15216
Phone: (412) 388-1140

#132
Scratch Food & Beverage
Cuisines: Cocktail Bar, Comfort Food, American
Average price: Modest
Area: Troy Hill
Address: 1720 Lowrie St
Pittsburgh, PA 15212
Phone: (412) 251-0822

#133
James Street Gastropub & Speakeasy
Cuisines: Gastropub, Jazz & Blues, American
Average price: Modest
Area: North Side
Address: 422 Foreland St
Pittsburgh, PA 15212
Phone: (412) 904-3335

#134
Mercurio's
Cuisines: Pizza, Gelato
Average price: Modest
Area: Shadyside
Address: 5523 Walnut St
Pittsburgh, PA 15232
Phone: (412) 621-6220

#135
Parker's PGH
Cuisines: Sandwiches, Bagels
Average price: Inexpensive
Area: Dormont
Address: 2911 Glenmore Ave
Pittsburgh, PA 15216
Phone: (412) 906-8007

#136
North Shore Deli
Cuisines: Deli
Average price: Inexpensive
Area: North Side
Address: 539 E Ohio St
Pittsburgh, PA 15212
Phone: (412) 231-2812

#137
Dijlah Restaurant
Cuisines: Middle Eastern, Hookah Bar, Breakfast & Brunch
Average price: Modest
Area: Lawrenceville
Address: 4130 Butler St
Pittsburgh, PA 15201
Phone: (412) 742-4998

#138
Aladdin's Eatery
Cuisines: Mediterranean, Vegetarian, Vegan
Average price: Modest
Area: Squirrel Hill
Address: 5878 Forbes Ave
Pittsburgh, PA 15217
Phone: (412) 421-5100

#139
Dive Bar & Grill
Cuisines: Dive Bar, American
Average price: Modest
Area: Lawrenceville
Address: 5147 Butler St
Pittsburgh, PA 15201
Phone: (412) 408-2015

#140
Waffles Incaffeinated
Cuisines: Breakfast & Brunch, Waffles
Average price: Modest
Area: South Side
Address: 2517 E Carson St
Pittsburgh, PA 15203
Phone: (412) 301-1763

#141
Sausalido
Cuisines: European, American
Average price: Modest
Area: Bloomfield
Address: 4621 Liberty Ave
Pittsburgh, PA 15224
Phone: (412) 683-4575

#142
Benjamins Western Ave Burger Bar
Cuisines: Burgers, Gastropub
Average price: Modest
Area: North Side
Address: 900 Western Ave
Pittsburgh, PA 15233
Phone: (412) 224-2163

#143
Birmingham Bridge Tavern
Cuisines: Bar, Barbeque
Average price: Modest
Area: South Side
Address: 2901 Sarah St
Pittsburgh, PA 15203
Phone: (412) 381-2739

#144
Pizza Taglio
Cuisines: Pizza, Italian
Average price: Modest
Area: East Liberty
Address: 126 S Highland Ave
Pittsburgh, PA 15206
Phone: (412) 404-7410

#145
Peanut Butter Jelly Time
Cuisines: Sandwiches, Desserts
Average price: Inexpensive
Area: Bloomfield
Address: 4709 Liberty Ave
Pittsburgh, PA 15224
Phone: (412) 622-0225

#146
Kassab's
Cuisines: Mediterranean, Lebanese
Average price: Modest
Area: South Side
Address: 1207 E Carson St
Pittsburgh, PA 15203
Phone: (412) 381-1820

#147
The Library
Cuisines: American
Average price: Modest
Area: South Side
Address: 2302 E Carson St
Pittsburgh, PA 15203
Phone: (412) 381-0517

#148
Joe & Pie
Cuisines: Pizza, Sandwiches
Average price: Inexpensive
Area: Downtown
Address: 955 Liberty Ave
Pittsburgh, PA 15222
Phone: (412) 402-0444

#149
Spak Brothers Pizza and More
Cuisines: Pizza, Salad
Average price: Inexpensive
Area: Garfield
Address: 5107 Penn Ave
Pittsburgh, PA 15224
Phone: (412) 362-7725

#150
Little Bangkok In the Strip
Cuisines: Thai
Average price: Modest
Area: Strip District
Address: 1906 Penn Ave
Pittsburgh, PA 15222
Phone: (412) 586-4107

#151
La Feria
Cuisines: Latin American, Peruvian
Average price: Modest
Area: Shadyside
Address: 5527 Walnut St
Pittsburgh, PA 15232
Phone: (412) 682-4501

#152
Independent Brewing Company
Cuisines: American, Pub, Beer Bar
Average price: Modest
Area: Squirrel Hill
Address: 1704 Shady Ave
Pittsburgh, PA 15217
Phone: (412) 422-5040

#153
E Town Bar and Grille
Cuisines: American
Average price: Inexpensive
Area: Etna
Address: 304 Butler St
Pittsburgh, PA 15223
Phone: (412) 784-1720

#154
Pitaland
Cuisines: Bakery, Cafe
Average price: Inexpensive
Area: Brookline
Address: 620 Brookline Blvd
Pittsburgh, PA 15226
Phone: (412) 531-5040

#155
Waffallonia
Cuisines: Desserts, Ice Cream
Average price: Inexpensive
Area: Squirrel Hill
Address: 1707 Murray Ave
Pittsburgh, PA 15217
Phone: (412) 521-4902

#156
Naya Cuisine
Cuisines: Middle Eastern, Diner
Average price: Modest
Area: Squirrel Hill
Address: 2018 Murray Ave
Pittsburgh, PA 15217
Phone: (412) 421-1920

Pittsburgh Restaurant Guide 2018 / Restaurants, Bars & Cafés

#157
Thin Man Sandwich Shop
Cuisines: Sandwiches
Average price: Inexpensive
Area: Strip District
Address: 50 21st St
Pittsburgh, PA 15222
Phone: (412) 586-7370

#158
Alfred's Deli & Market
Cuisines: Deli, Polish, Grocery
Average price: Inexpensive
Area: Polish Hill
Address: 3041 Brereton St
Pittsburgh, PA 15219
Phone: (412) 682-3100

#159
Pittsburgh Barbecue Company
Cuisines: Barbeque, Caterer
Average price: Modest
Area: Banksville
Address: 1000 Banksville Rd
Pittsburgh, PA 15216
Phone: (412) 563-1005

#160
Salem's Market & Grill
Cuisines: Meat Shops, Butcher, Chicken Shop
Average price: Inexpensive
Area: Strip District
Address: 2923 Penn Ave
Pittsburgh, PA 15201
Phone: (412) 235-7828

#161
Thai Spoon
Cuisines: Thai
Average price: Modest
Area: Dormont
Address: 1409 Potomac Ave
Pittsburgh, PA 15216
Phone: (412) 563-1409

#162
Bea Taco Town
Cuisines: Mexican
Average price: Inexpensive
Area: Banksville
Address: 2957 Banksville Rd
Pittsburgh, PA 15216
Phone: (412) 344-1122

#163
Peppi's
Cuisines: Burgers
Average price: Inexpensive
Area: Strip District
Address: 1721 Penn Ave
Pittsburgh, PA 15222
Phone: (412) 562-0125

#164
Murray Avenue Grill
Cuisines: American
Average price: Modest
Area: Squirrel Hill
Address: 1720 Murray Ave
Pittsburgh, PA 15217
Phone: (412) 521-1272

#165
Bangal Kabab House and Restaurant
Cuisines: Indian, Bangladeshi
Average price: Modest
Area: Oakland
Address: 320 Atwood St
Pittsburgh, PA 15213
Phone: (412) 605-0521

#166
Winghart's Burger & Whiskey Bar
Cuisines: Burgers, Pizza, Whiskey Bar
Average price: Modest
Area: South Side
Address: 1505 E Carson St
Pittsburgh, PA 15203
Phone: (412) 904-4620

#167
Sukhothai Bistro
Cuisines: Thai
Average price: Modest
Area: Squirrel Hill
Address: 5813 Forbes Ave
Pittsburgh, PA 15217
Phone: (412) 521-8989

#168
Coca Cafe
Cuisines: Breakfast & Brunch, American
Average price: Modest
Area: Lawrenceville
Address: 3811 Butler St
Pittsburgh, PA 15201
Phone: (412) 621-3171

#169
Benny Fierro's
Cuisines: Pizza
Average price: Inexpensive
Area: South Side
Address: 1906 E Carson St.
Pittsburgh, PA 15203
Phone: (412) 709-6077

#170
Tootie's Famous Italian Beef
Cuisines: American, Sandwiches
Average price: Inexpensive
Area: South Side
Address: 93 S 16th St
Pittsburgh, PA 15203
Phone: (412) 586-5959

#171
Hello Bistro
Cuisines: American
Average price: Inexpensive
Area: Oakland
Address: 3605 Forbes Ave
Pittsburgh, PA 15213
Phone: (412) 687-8787

#172
Make Your Mark
Cuisines: Coffee & Tea, Sandwiches
Average price: Inexpensive
Area: Point Breeze
Address: 6736 Reynolds St
Pittsburgh, PA 15206
Phone: (412) 365-2117

#173
The Yard Gastropub
Cuisines: American, Gastropub, Burgers
Average price: Modest
Area: Shadyside
Address: 736 Bellefonte St
Pittsburgh, PA 15232
Phone: (412) 709-6351

#174
Joseph Tambellini Restaurant
Cuisines: Italian
Average price: Expensive
Area: Highland Park
Address: 5701 Bryant St
Pittsburgh, PA 15206
Phone: (412) 665-9000

#175
Bistro To Go
Cuisines: Salad, American, Sandwiches, Southern
Average price: Modest
Area: North Side
Address: 415 E Ohio St
Pittsburgh, PA 15212
Phone: (412) 231-0218

#176
Groceria Merante
Cuisines: Grocery, Sandwiches
Average price: Inexpensive
Area: Oakland
Address: 3454 Bates St
Pittsburgh, PA 15213
Phone: (412) 683-3924

#177
Hunan Bar
Cuisines: Szechuan
Average price: Modest
Area: Oakland
Address: 239 Atwood St
Pittsburgh, PA 15213
Phone: (412) 621-2326

#178
Revel + Roost
Cuisines: Bar, American
Average price: Modest
Area: Downtown
Address: 242 Forbes Ave
Pittsburgh, PA 15222
Phone: (412) 281-1134

#179
Salim's Middle Eastern Food Store
Cuisines: Deli, Imported Food
Average price: Inexpensive
Area: Bloomfield
Address: 4705 Centre Ave
Pittsburgh, PA 15213
Phone: (412) 621-8110

#180
BFG Café
Cuisines: Pizza, Greek, Mediterranean
Average price: Inexpensive
Area: Garfield, Bloomfield
Address: 5335 Penn Ave
Pittsburgh, PA 15224
Phone: (412) 661-2345

#181
STACK'D Burgers & Beer
Cuisines: Burgers, Pub, American
Average price: Modest
Area: Shadyside
Address: 728 Copeland St
Pittsburgh, PA 15232
Phone: (412) 682-3354

#182
Los Cabos Mexican Restaurant
Cuisines: Mexican
Average price: Inexpensive
Area: Lawrenceville
Address: 4108-10 Penn Ave
Pittsburgh, PA 15224
Phone: (412) 251-5105

#183
Vue 412
Cuisines: American
Average price: Modest
Area: Duquesne Heights, Mt. Washington
Address: 1200 Grandview Ave
Pittsburgh, PA 15211
Phone: (412) 381-1919

#184
Industry Public House
Cuisines: American, Cocktail Bar
Average price: Modest
Area: Lawrenceville
Address: 4305 Butler St
Pittsburgh, PA 15201
Phone: (412) 683-1100

#185
Casbah
Cuisines: Mediterranean, Wine Bar, Diner
Average price: Expensive
Area: Shadyside
Address: 229 S Highland Ave
Pittsburgh, PA 15206
Phone: (412) 661-5656

#186
Penn Brewery
Cuisines: German, Breweries, Venue & Event Space
Average price: Modest
Area: Troy Hill
Address: 800 Vinial St
Pittsburgh, PA 15212
Phone: (412) 237-9400

#187
Bea Taco Town
Cuisines: Mexican
Average price: Inexpensive
Area: Downtown
Address: 633 Smithfield St
Pittsburgh, PA 15222
Phone: (412) 471-8361

#188
Angkor Restaurant
Cuisines: Cambodian, Thai
Average price: Modest
Area: West End
Address: 2350 Noblestown Rd
Pittsburgh, PA 15205
Phone: (412) 928-8424

#189
Istanbul Grille
Cuisines: Turkish, Imported Food
Average price: Inexpensive
Area: Downtown
Address: 600 Grant St
Pittsburgh, PA 15219
Phone: (412) 999-0841

#190
Pamela's
Cuisines: Breakfast & Brunch, Diner
Average price: Inexpensive
Area: Millvale
Address: 232 North Ave
Pittsburgh, PA 15209
Phone: (412) 821-4655

#191
The Fire Side Public House
Cuisines: American, Gastropub, Sandwiches
Average price: Modest
Area: East Liberty
Address: 6290 Broad Street
Pittsburgh, PA 15206
Phone: (412) 661-9900

#192
Sonoma Grille
Cuisines: American, Tapas Bar
Average price: Expensive
Area: Downtown
Address: 947 Penn Ave
Pittsburgh, PA 15289
Phone: (412) 697-1336

#193
Cioppino
Cuisines: Seafood, Steakhouse
Average price: Expensive
Area: Strip District
Address: 2350 Railroad St
Pittsburgh, PA 15222
Phone: (412) 281-6593

#194
Primanti Bros.
Cuisines: Sandwiches, American, Sports Bar
Average price: Inexpensive
Area: Downtown
Address: 2 South Market Sq
Pittsburgh, PA 15222
Phone: (412) 261-1599

#195
Randita's Organic Vegan Cafe
Cuisines: Vegan
Average price: Modest
Area: Aspinwall
Address: 207 Commercial Ave
Pittsburgh, PA 15215
Phone: (412) 408-3907

#196
Krista's Cantina
Cuisines: Bar, Pool Hall, Chicken Wings
Average price: Inexpensive
Area: North Side
Address: 2650 California Ave
Pittsburgh, PA 15212
Phone: (412) 766-1676

#197
Union Pig & Chicken
Cuisines: Barbeque, Bar
Average price: Modest
Area: East Liberty
Address: 220 N Highland Ave
Pittsburgh, PA 15206
Phone: (412) 363-7675

#198
P&G's Pamela's Diner
Cuisines: Diner, Breakfast & Brunch
Average price: Inexpensive
Area: Strip District
Address: 60 21 St
Pittsburgh, PA 15222
Phone: (412) 281-6366

#199
Girasole Restaurant
Cuisines: Italian
Average price: Modest
Area: Shadyside
Address: 733 Copeland St
Pittsburgh, PA 15232
Phone: (412) 682-2130

#200
Remedy
Cuisines: Bar, American
Average price: Inexpensive
Area: Lawrenceville
Address: 5121 Butler St
Pittsburgh, PA 15201
Phone: (412) 781-6771

#201
BRGR
Cuisines: Burgers, American
Average price: Modest
Area: Shadyside
Address: 5997 Centre Ave
Pittsburgh, PA 15206
Phone: (412) 362-2333

#202
Whitfield
Cuisines: American
Average price: Expensive
Area: East Liberty
Address: 120 S Whitfield St
Pittsburgh, PA 15206
Phone: (412) 626-3090

#203
Shady Grove
Cuisines: American
Average price: Modest
Area: Shadyside
Address: 5500 Walnut St
Pittsburgh, PA 15232
Phone: (412) 697-0909

#204
Chicken Latino
Cuisines: Latin American, Peruvian
Average price: Inexpensive
Area: Strip District
Address: 155 21st St
Pittsburgh, PA 15222
Phone: (412) 246-0974

#205
Pan
Cuisines: Asian Fusion
Average price: Modest
Area: Lawrenceville
Address: 3519 Butler St
Pittsburgh, PA 15201
Phone: (412) 944-2975

#206
Pho Minh
Cuisines: Vietnamese
Average price: Inexpensive
Area: Garfield
Address: 4917 Penn Ave
Pittsburgh, PA 15224
Phone: (412) 661-7443

#207
Braddock's Pittsburgh Brasserie
Cuisines: American
Average price: Modest
Area: Downtown
Address: 107 6th St
Pittsburgh, PA 15222
Phone: (412) 992-2005

#208
Rose Tea Café
Cuisines: Taiwanese, Bubble Tea, Cafe
Average price: Modest
Area: Squirrel Hill
Address: 5874 1/2 Forbes Ave
Pittsburgh, PA 15217
Phone: (412) 421-2238

#209
Cafe Moulin
Cuisines: Breakfast & Brunch, French, Coffee & Tea
Average price: Modest
Area: Shadyside
Address: 732 Filbert Street
Pittsburgh, PA 15232
Phone: (412) 347-8508

#210
Lot 17
Cuisines: American, Bar
Average price: Modest
Area: Bloomfield
Address: 4617 Liberty Ave
Pittsburgh, PA 15224
Phone: (412) 687-8117

#211
Sidelines Bar & Grill
Cuisines: Dive Bar, American
Average price: Modest
Area: Millvale
Address: 621 Evergreen Ave
Pittsburgh, PA 15209
Phone: (412) 821-4492

#212
How Lee Chinese Food
Cuisines: Chinese
Average price: Modest
Area: Squirrel Hill
Address: 5888 Forbes Ave
Pittsburgh, PA 15217
Phone: (412) 422-1888

#213
NU Jewish Bistro
Cuisines: American, Deli, Sandwiches
Average price: Modest
Area: Squirrel Hill
Address: 1711 Murray Ave
Pittsburgh, PA 15217
Phone: (412) 422-0220

#214
La Tavola Italiana
Cuisines: Pizza, Italian
Average price: Modest
Area: Mt. Washington
Address: 1 Boggs Ave
Pittsburgh, PA 15211
Phone: (412) 481-6627

#215
Geppetto Cafe
Cuisines: Coffee & Tea, Breakfast & Brunch
Average price: Modest
Area: Lawrenceville
Address: 4121 Butler St
Pittsburgh, PA 15201
Phone: (412) 709-6399

#216
Kickback Pinball Cafe
Cuisines: Arcades, Cafe
Average price: Inexpensive
Area: Lawrenceville
Address: 4326 Butler St
Pittsburgh, PA 15201
Phone: (412) 536-5211

Pittsburgh Restaurant Guide 2018 / Restaurants, Bars & Cafés

#217
Round Corner Cantina
Cuisines: Mexican, Bar, Dance Club
Average price: Modest
Area: Lawrenceville
Address: 3720 Butler St
Pittsburgh, PA 15201
Phone: (412) 904-2279

#218
Chick'n Bubbly
Cuisines: Korean, Bubble Tea, Chicken Wings
Average price: Inexpensive
Area: Oakland
Address: 117 Oakland Ave
Pittsburgh, PA 15213
Phone: (412) 863-7741

#219
Sushi Fuku
Cuisines: Sushi Bar, Japanese
Average price: Inexpensive
Area: Oakland
Address: 120 Oakland Ave
Pittsburgh, PA 15213
Phone: (412) 687-3858

#220
Leon's Caribbean Restaurant
Cuisines: Caribbean, Seafood
Average price: Inexpensive
Area: Allentown
Address: 823 E Warrington Ave
Pittsburgh, PA 15210
Phone: (412) 431-5366

#221
Mad Mex - Shadyside
Cuisines: Mexican, Tex-Mex
Average price: Modest
Area: Shadyside
Address: 220 S Highland Ave
Pittsburgh, PA 15206
Phone: (412) 345-0185

#222
Robert Wholey and Co Fish Market
Cuisines: Grocery, Seafood Market, Seafood
Average price: Modest
Area: Strip District
Address: 1711 Penn Ave
Pittsburgh, PA 15222
Phone: (412) 391-3737

#223
La Gondola Pizzeria & Restaurant
Cuisines: Italian
Average price: Inexpensive
Area: Downtown
Address: 4 Market Sq
Pittsburgh, PA 15222
Phone: (412) 261-5252

#224
Ramen Bar
Cuisines: Ramen
Average price: Modest
Area: Squirrel Hill
Address: 5860 Forbes Ave
Pittsburgh, PA 15217
Phone: (412) 521-5138

#225
Double Wide Grill
Cuisines: Barbeque, Vegetarian, American
Average price: Modest
Area: South Side
Address: 2339 E Carson St
Pittsburgh, PA 15203
Phone: (412) 390-1111

#226
Moonlite Cafe
Cuisines: Italian
Average price: Modest
Area: Brookline
Address: 530 Brookline Blvd
Pittsburgh, PA 15226
Phone: (412) 531-2811

#227
Adolfo's Restaurant
Cuisines: Latin American, Italian
Average price: Modest
Area: Bloomfield
Address: 4770 Liberty Ave
Pittsburgh, PA 15224
Phone: (412) 681-0505

#228
Fiori's Pizzaria
Cuisines: Pizza, Italian
Average price: Inexpensive
Area: Beechview
Address: 103 Capital Ave
Pittsburgh, PA 15226
Phone: (412) 343-7788

#229
Squirrel Hill Cafe
Cuisines: Pub, American
Average price: Inexpensive
Area: Squirrel Hill
Address: 5802 Forbes Ave
Pittsburgh, PA 15217
Phone: (412) 521-3327

#230
Yovi's
Cuisines: Fast Food, Hot Dogs, Sandwiches
Average price: Inexpensive
Area: Downtown
Address: 477 Graeme St Market Sq
Pittsburgh, PA 15222
Phone: (412) 628-4943

#231
Harris Grill
Cuisines: American, Bar, Diner
Average price: Modest
Area: Shadyside
Address: 5747 Ellsworth Ave
Pittsburgh, PA 15232
Phone: (412) 362-5273

#232
S&D Polish Deli
Cuisines: Polish
Average price: Inexpensive
Area: Strip District
Address: 2204 Penn Ave
Pittsburgh, PA 15222
Phone: (412) 281-2906

#233
Eddie Merlot's - Pittsburgh
Cuisines: Seafood, Steakhouse, Salad
Average price: Expensive
Area: Downtown
Address: 444 Liberty Ave
Pittsburgh, PA 15222
Phone: (412) 235-7676

#234
Pints On Penn
Cuisines: American, American, Pub
Average price: Modest
Area: Lawrenceville
Address: 3523 Penn Ave
Pittsburgh, PA 15201
Phone: (412) 945-7468

#235
Umi
Cuisines: Japanese
Average price: Exclusive
Area: Shadyside
Address: 5847 Ellsworth Ave
Pittsburgh, PA 15232
Phone: (412) 362-6198

#236
Pastoli's Pizza, Pasta & Paisans
Cuisines: Pizza, Gluten-Free
Average price: Modest
Area: Squirrel Hill
Address: 1900 Murray Ave
Pittsburgh, PA 15217
Phone: (412) 422-9660

#237
Pizzaiolo Primo
Cuisines: Italian, Wine Bar, Pizza
Average price: Modest
Area: Downtown
Address: 8 Market Sq
Pittsburgh, PA 15222
Phone: (412) 307-5263

#238
Two Louie's Market
Cuisines: Sandwiches
Average price: Inexpensive
Area: Strip District
Address: 1233 Penn Ave
Pittsburgh, PA 15222
Phone: (412) 586-5593

#239
Cafe Sam
Cuisines: American
Average price: Modest
Area: Bloomfield
Address: 5242 Baum Blvd
Pittsburgh, PA 15224
Phone: (412) 621-2000

#240
Zarra's A Taste of Southern Italy
Cuisines: Italian
Average price: Modest
Area: Oakland
Address: 3887 Bigelow Blvd
Pittsburgh, PA 15213
Phone: (412) 682-8296

#241
The BeerHive
Cuisines: American, Bar
Average price: Modest
Area: Strip District
Address: 2117 Penn Ave
Pittsburgh, PA 15222
Phone: (412) 904-4502

#242
My Thai
Cuisines: Thai
Average price: Modest
Area: Dormont
Address: 3024 W Liberty Ave
Pittsburgh, PA 15216
Phone: (412) 207-7507

#243
Cucina Vitale
Cuisines: Italian, Breakfast & Brunch
Average price: Modest
Area: South Side
Address: 2516 E Carson St
Pittsburgh, PA 15203
Phone: (412) 481-8000

#244
The Dream BBQ
Cuisines: Barbeque
Average price: Modest
Area: Homewood
Address: 7600 N Braddock Ave
Pittsburgh, PA 15208
Phone: (412) 244-0355

#245
The Capital Grille
Cuisines: Steakhouse, Seafood, Wine Bar
Average price: Exclusive
Area: Downtown
Address: 301 5th Ave
Pittsburgh, PA 15222
Phone: (412) 338-9100

#246
Pizza Perfectta
Cuisines: Pizza
Average price: Modest
Area: Shadyside
Address: 258 S Highland Ave
Pittsburgh, PA 15206
Phone: (412) 661-9991

#247
Ginza
Cuisines: Japanese, Sushi Bar
Average price: Modest
Area: Bloomfield
Address: 4734 Liberty Ave
Pittsburgh, PA 15224
Phone: (412) 688-7272

#248
Don's Diner
Cuisines: Diner
Average price: Inexpensive
Area: North Side
Address: 1729 Eckert St
Pittsburgh, PA 15212
Phone: (412) 761-5883

#249
Nak Won Garden
Cuisines: Korean
Average price: Modest
Area: Friendship, Shadyside
Address: 5504 Centre Ave
Pittsburgh, PA 15232
Phone: (412) 904-4635

#250
Bella Notte
Cuisines: Pizza, Italian
Average price: Modest
Area: Strip District
Address: 1914 Penn Ave
Pittsburgh, PA 15222
Phone: (412) 281-4488

#251
Six Penn Kitchen
Cuisines: American
Average price: Modest
Area: Downtown
Address: 146 6th St
Pittsburgh, PA 15222
Phone: (412) 566-7366

#252
Grandview Saloon
Cuisines: Steakhouse, Seafood, Wine Bar
Average price: Modest
Area: Duquesne Heights
Address: 1212 Grandview Ave
Pittsburgh, PA 15211
Phone: (412) 431-1400

#253
Uncle Sam's Submarines
Cuisines: Sandwiches
Average price: Inexpensive
Area: Oakland
Address: 210 Oakland Ave
Pittsburgh, PA 15213
Phone: (412) 621-1885

#254
Top Shabu-Shabu & Lounge
Cuisines: Hot Pot, Chinese, Japanese
Average price: Modest
Area: Oakland
Address: 114 Atwood St
Pittsburgh, PA 15213
Phone: (412) 879-1555

#255
Grand Concourse
Cuisines: Seafood, Breakfast & Brunch
Average price: Expensive
Area: South Side
Address: 100 West Station Square Dr
Pittsburgh, PA 15219
Phone: (412) 261-1717

#256
Grant Bar
Cuisines: American
Average price: Modest
Area: Millvale
Address: 114 Grant Ave
Pittsburgh, PA 15209
Phone: (412) 821-1541

#257
Carson Street Deli & Craft Beer Bar
Cuisines: Deli, Bar, Sandwiches
Average price: Inexpensive
Area: South Side
Address: 1507 E Carson St
Pittsburgh, PA 15203
Phone: (412) 381-5335

#258
Z-Best BBQ
Cuisines: Barbeque
Average price: Inexpensive
Area: The Hill District
Address: 1315 5th Ave
Pittsburgh, PA 15219
Phone: (412) 235-7163

#259
The Real McCoy Sandwich Shop
Cuisines: Sandwiches
Average price: Inexpensive
Area: South Side
Address: 1301 E Carson St
Pittsburgh, PA 15203
Phone: (412) 481-0566

#260
Olive or Twist
Cuisines: American, Lounge, Cocktail Bar
Average price: Modest
Area: Downtown
Address: 140 6th St
Pittsburgh, PA 15222
Phone: (412) 255-0525

#261
Sushi & Rolls
Cuisines: Sushi Bar
Average price: Inexpensive
Area: Downtown
Address: 301 Grant St
Pittsburgh, PA 15219
Phone: (412) 255-0520

#262
The Yard
Cuisines: American, Gastropub
Average price: Modest
Area: Downtown
Address: 100 5th Ave
Pittsburgh, PA 15222
Phone: (412) 291-8182

#263
Smoq Pitt
Cuisines: Barbeque
Average price: Modest
Area: Brookline
Address: 600 Brookline Blvd
Pittsburgh, PA 15226
Phone: (412) 618-4672

#264
Sharp Edge
Cuisines: Belgian, American, Pub
Average price: Modest
Area: Downtown
Address: 922 Penn Ave
Pittsburgh, PA 15222
Phone: (412) 338-2437

#265
Mad Mex - Oakland
Cuisines: Tex-Mex, Mexican
Average price: Modest
Area: Oakland
Address: 370 Atwood St
Pittsburgh, PA 15213
Phone: (412) 681-5656

#266
Jolina's Mediterranean Cuisine
Cuisines: Mediterranean, Middle Eastern, Soup
Average price: Modest
Area: Brookline
Address: 1011 Brookline Blvd
Pittsburgh, PA 15226
Phone: (412) 341-3333

#267
Primanti Bros.
Cuisines: Sandwiches, American, Sports Bar
Average price: Inexpensive
Area: Oakland
Address: 3803 Forbes Ave
Pittsburgh, PA 15213
Phone: (412) 621-4444

#268
Hello Bistro
Cuisines: Salad, Cafe, Burgers
Average price: Inexpensive
Area: South Side
Address: 1922 E Carson St
Pittsburgh, PA 15203
Phone: (412) 390-1922

#269
Mixtape
Cuisines: Dance Club, Venue & Event Space
Average price: Modest
Area: Garfield
Address: 4907 Penn Ave
Pittsburgh, PA 15224
Phone: (412) 661-1727

#270
Ephesus Mediterranean Kitchen
Cuisines: Pizza
Average price: Modest
Area: Downtown
Address: 219 4th Ave
Pittsburgh, PA 15222
Phone: (412) 552-9020

#271
Reyna Foods
Cuisines: Grocery, Mexican
Average price: Inexpensive
Area: Strip District
Address: 2023 Penn Ave
Pittsburgh, PA 15222
Phone: (412) 261-2606

#272
Mezzo
Cuisines: Italian
Average price: Modest
Area: Downtown
Address: 942 Penn Avenue
Pittsburgh, PA 15222
Phone: (412) 281-2810

#273
South Side BBQ Company
Cuisines: Food Truck, Barbeque
Average price: Modest
Area: South Side
Address: 75 S 17th St
Pittsburgh, PA 15203
Phone: (412) 381-4566

#274
Mattress Factory Café
Cuisines: American
Average price: Inexpensive
Area: North Side
Address: 500 Sampsonia Way
Pittsburgh, PA 15212
Phone: (412) 231-3169

#275
Lidia's
Cuisines: Italian, Bar
Average price: Expensive
Area: Strip District
Address: 1400 Smallman St
Pittsburgh, PA 15222
Phone: (412) 552-0150

#276
Feng Japanese Steak Hibachi & Sushi House
Cuisines: Sushi Bar, Teppanyaki
Average price: Modest
Area: Bloomfield
Address: 4305 Main St
Pittsburgh, PA 15224
Phone: (412) 688-8800

#277
P&G's Pamela's Diner
Cuisines: Breakfast & Brunch
Average price: Inexpensive
Area: Shadyside
Address: 5527 Walnut St
Pittsburgh, PA 15232
Phone: (412) 683-1003

#278
Hokkaido Seafood Buffet
Cuisines: Buffet, Sushi Bar, Japanese
Average price: Modest
Area: Squirrel Hill
Address: 4612 Browns Hill Rd
Pittsburgh, PA 15217
Phone: (412) 421-1422

#279
Kelly O's Diner
Cuisines: Diner, Breakfast & Brunch
Average price: Inexpensive
Area: Strip District
Address: 2400 Smallman St
Pittsburgh, PA 15222
Phone: (412) 232-3447

#280
Chaya Japanese Cuisine
Cuisines: Japanese, Sushi Bar, Soup
Average price: Modest
Area: Squirrel Hill
Address: 2032 Murray Ave
Pittsburgh, PA 15217
Phone: (412) 422-2082

#281
The Abbey on Butler
Cuisines: Bar, Cafe, American
Average price: Modest
Area: Lawrenceville
Address: 4635 Butler Street
Pittsburgh, PA 15201
Phone: (412) 682-0200

#282
Tavern 245
Cuisines: American
Average price: Modest
Area: Downtown
Address: 245 Fourth Ave
Pittsburgh, PA 15222
Phone: (412) 281-4345

#283
Casa Reyna
Cuisines: Mexican
Average price: Modest
Area: Strip District
Address: 2031 Penn Ave
Pittsburgh, PA 15222
Phone: (412) 904-1242

#284
Chateau Café & Cakery
Cuisines: Cafe, Coffee & Tea, Bakery
Average price: Inexpensive
Area: North Side
Address: 1501 Preble Ave
Pittsburgh, PA 15233
Phone: (412) 802-2537

#285
Pamela's Upstreet Diner
Cuisines: Breakfast & Brunch, Diner
Average price: Inexpensive
Area: Squirrel Hill
Address: 1711 Murray Ave
Pittsburgh, PA 15217
Phone: (412) 422-9457

#286
Tipsy Cow
Cuisines: Burgers, Bar, American
Average price: Modest
Area: Shadyside
Address: 5741 Ellsworth Ave
Pittsburgh, PA 15232
Phone: (412) 404-8409

#287
The Mediterranean Grill
Cuisines: Mediterranean, Lebanese
Average price: Modest
Area: Squirrel Hill
Address: 5824 Forbes Ave
Pittsburgh, PA 15217
Phone: (412) 521-5505

#288
Local Bar + Kitchen
Cuisines: Bar, American, Breakfast & Brunch
Average price: Modest
Area: South Side
Address: 1515 E Carson St
Pittsburgh, PA 15203
Phone: (412) 308-5183

#289
Living Juicy
Cuisines: Juice Bar, Cafe
Average price: Inexpensive
Area: Shadyside
Address: 5892 Ellsworth Ave
Pittsburgh, PA 15232
Phone: (412) 361-0361

#290
Green Pepper
Cuisines: Karaoke, Korean
Average price: Modest
Area: Squirrel Hill
Address: 2020 Murray Ave
Pittsburgh, PA 15217
Phone: (412) 422-2277

#291
Café Cravings
Cuisines: Cafe, Sandwiches
Average price: Inexpensive
Area: Mt. Washington
Address: 402 Bigham St
Pittsburgh, PA 15211
Phone: (412) 481-2700

#292
Paris 66
Cuisines: French, Gluten-Free, Brasserie
Average price: Modest
Area: Shadyside
Address: 6018 Centre Ave
Pittsburgh, PA 15206
Phone: (412) 404-8166

#293
Wilson's Bar-B-Q
Cuisines: Barbeque
Average price: Modest
Area: North Side
Address: 700 N Taylor Ave
Pittsburgh, PA 15212
Phone: (412) 322-7427

#294
Diamond Market Bar & Grill
Cuisines: Bar, American
Average price: Modest
Area: Downtown
Address: 430 Market St
Pittsburgh, PA 15222
Phone: (412) 325-2000

#295
Istanbul Grille
Cuisines: Turkish
Average price: Inexpensive
Area: Downtown
Address: 339 Sixth Ave
Pittsburgh, PA 15215
Phone: (412) 316-0092

#296
Pizza Milano
Cuisines: Pizza
Average price: Modest
Area: The Hill District
Address: 1304 5th Ave
Pittsburgh, PA 15219
Phone: (412) 281-8181

#297
The Zenith
Cuisines: Vegetarian, Salad, Vegan
Average price: Modest
Area: South Side
Address: 86 S 26th St
Pittsburgh, PA 15203
Phone: (412) 481-4833

#298
Soba
Cuisines: Asian Fusion, Japanese, Korean
Average price: Expensive
Area: Shadyside
Address: 5847 Ellsworth Ave
Pittsburgh, PA 15232
Phone: (412) 362-5656

#299
Ten Penny
Cuisines: American
Average price: Modest
Area: Downtown
Address: 960 Penn Ave
Pittsburgh, PA 15222
Phone: (412) 318-8000

#300
Thai Cuisine
Cuisines: Thai
Average price: Modest
Area: Bloomfield
Address: 4627 Liberty Ave
Pittsburgh, PA 15224
Phone: (412) 688-9661

#301
All India
Cuisines: Indian
Average price: Modest
Area: Oakland
Address: 315 N Craig St
Pittsburgh, PA 15213
Phone: (412) 681-6600

#302
OTB Bicycle Café
Cuisines: American, Beer, Wine & Spirits
Average price: Modest
Area: South Side
Address: 2518 E Carson St
Pittsburgh, PA 15203
Phone: (412) 381-3698

#303
Dinette
Cuisines: Pizza
Average price: Modest
Area: Shadyside
Address: 5996 Centre Ave
Pittsburgh, PA 15206
Phone: (412) 362-0202

#304
La Gourmandine Bakery & Pastry Shop
Cuisines: Bakery, French
Average price: Inexpensive
Area: Lawrenceville
Address: 4605 Butler St
Pittsburgh, PA 15201
Phone: (412) 682-2210

#305
Caliente Pizza & Draft House
Cuisines: Pizza
Average price: Modest
Area: Bloomfield
Address: 4624 Liberty Ave
Pittsburgh, PA 15224
Phone: (412) 682-1414

#306
Thai Hana
Cuisines: Thai, Sushi Bar, Japanese
Average price: Modest
Area: Oakland
Address: 3608 5th Ave
Pittsburgh, PA 15213
Phone: (412) 621-1100

#307
SoHo
Cuisines: American
Average price: Modest
Area: North Side
Address: 203 Federal St
Pittsburgh, PA 15212
Phone: (412) 321-7646

#308
Craftwork Kitchen
Cuisines: Food Court
Average price: Inexpensive
Area: Downtown
Address: 600 Grant St
Pittsburgh, PA 15219
Phone: (412) 281-1460

#309
Mullin's Diner
Cuisines: American
Average price: Inexpensive
Area: North Side
Address: 876 Progress St
Pittsburgh, PA 15212
Phone: (412) 231-7084

#310
Chengdu Gourmet
Cuisines: Chinese, Seafood, Soup
Average price: Modest
Area: Squirrel Hill
Address: 5840 Forward Ave
Pittsburgh, PA 15217
Phone: (412) 521-2088

#311
Social
Cuisines: American, Gastropub
Average price: Modest
Area: Shadyside
Address: 6425 Penn Ave
Pittsburgh, PA 15206
Phone: (412) 362-1234

#312
Luke and Mike's Frontporch
Cuisines: American
Average price: Modest
Area: Aspinwall
Address: 235 Commercial Ave
Pittsburgh, PA 15215
Phone: (412) 252-2877

#313
Le Mont
Cuisines: American, Diner, Lounge
Average price: Expensive
Area: Mt. Washington
Address: 1114 Grandview Ave
Pittsburgh, PA 15211
Phone: (412) 431-3100

#314
Kiku Japanese Restaurant
Cuisines: Japanese, Sushi Bar
Average price: Modest
Area: South Side
Address: 225 W Station Square Dr
Pittsburgh, PA 15219
Phone: (412) 765-3200

#315
P&G's Pamela's Diner
Cuisines: Breakfast & Brunch
Average price: Inexpensive
Area: Oakland
Address: 3703 Forbes Ave
Pittsburgh, PA 15213
Phone: (412) 683-4066

#316
Stinky's Bar & Grill
Cuisines: American
Average price: Modest
Area: Lawrenceville
Address: 4901 Hatfield St
Pittsburgh, PA 15201
Phone: (412) 224-4301

#317
Uncle Sam's Submarines
Cuisines: Sandwiches
Average price: Inexpensive
Area: Squirrel Hill
Address: 5808 Forbes Ave
Pittsburgh, PA 15217
Phone: (412) 521-7827

#318
Giovanni's Pizza & Restaurant
Cuisines: Pizza
Average price: Modest
Area: The Hill District
Address: 1504 5th Ave
Pittsburgh, PA 15219
Phone: (412) 391-4955

#319
Mallorca Restaurant
Cuisines: Spanish, Basque, Tapas/Small Plates
Average price: Expensive
Area: South Side
Address: 2228 E Carson St
Pittsburgh, PA 15203
Phone: (412) 307-7030

#320
SAKE Asian Cuisine & Sushi Bar
Cuisines: Sushi Bar, Asian Fusion
Average price: Modest
Area: South Side
Address: 2773 Sidney St
Pittsburgh, PA 15203
Phone: (412) 481-8888

#321
Hello Bistro
Cuisines: Salad, American, Burgers
Average price: Inexpensive
Area: Downtown
Address: 292 Forbes Ave
Pittsburgh, PA 15222
Phone: (412) 434-0100

#322
Corner Mercantile
Cuisines: Desserts, Deli
Average price: Inexpensive
Area: Downtown
Address: 472 wood Street
Pittsburgh, PA 15222
Phone: (412) 586-5738

#323
Beta Bites
Cuisines: American, Moroccan, Sandwiches
Average price: Inexpensive
Area: Oakland
Address: 338 S Bouquet St
Pittsburgh, PA 15213
Phone: (412) 621-7000

#324
Ritters Diner
Cuisines: Diner, American, Breakfast & Brunch
Average price: Inexpensive
Area: Bloomfield
Address: 5221 Baum Blvd
Pittsburgh, PA 15224
Phone: (412) 682-4852

#325
Deli On North Avenue
Cuisines: Food, Deli
Average price: Inexpensive
Area: North Side
Address: 4 E North Ave
Pittsburgh, PA 15212
Phone: (412) 322-3354

#326
Arnold's Tea
Cuisines: Sandwiches, Desserts, Tea Room
Average price: Inexpensive
Area: North Side
Address: 502 E Ohio St
Pittsburgh, PA 15212
Phone: (412) 322-2494

#327
Fredos Deli
Cuisines: Deli, Sandwiches
Average price: Inexpensive
Area: Dormont
Address: 1451 Potomac Ave
Pittsburgh, PA 15216
Phone: (412) 344-1060

#328
Savoy
Cuisines: American, Wine Bar
Average price: Expensive
Area: Strip District
Address: 2623 Penn Ave
Pittsburgh, PA 15222
Phone: (412) 281-0660

#329
Smokin' Joe's
Cuisines: Bar, American
Average price: Inexpensive
Area: South Side
Address: 2001 E Carson St
Pittsburgh, PA 15203
Phone: (412) 431-6757

#330
City Oven
Cuisines: Pizza
Average price: Inexpensive
Area: Downtown
Address: 336 4th Ave
Pittsburgh, PA 15222
Phone: (412) 281-6836

#331
Rivertowne
Cuisines: American, Pub
Average price: Modest
Area: North Side
Address: 337 N Shore Dr
Pittsburgh, PA 15212
Phone: (412) 322-5000

#332
Bombay Gyro's and Lunch Box
Cuisines: Mediterranean, Imported Food
Average price: Inexpensive
Area: Downtown
Address: 212 10th St
Pittsburgh, PA 15215
Phone: (412) 434-0200

#333
Sun Penang
Cuisines: Malaysian
Average price: Modest
Area: Squirrel Hill
Address: 5829 Forbes Ave
Pittsburgh, PA 15217
Phone: (412) 421-7600

#334
Village Tavern and Trattoria
Cuisines: Italian
Average price: Modest
Area: West End
Address: 424 S Main St
Pittsburgh, PA 15220
Phone: (412) 458-0417

#335
The Huddle
Cuisines: Bar, American
Average price: Inexpensive
Area: Beechview
Address: 1648 Broadway Ave
Pittsburgh, PA 15216
Phone: (412) 344-6455

#336
The Pretzel Shop
Cuisines: American, Pretzels, Sandwiches
Average price: Inexpensive
Area: South Side
Address: 2316 E Carson St
Pittsburgh, PA 15203
Phone: (412) 431-2574

#337
Stack'd Burgers & Beer
Cuisines: American, Burgers, Bar
Average price: Modest
Area: Oakland
Address: 3716 Forbes Ave
Pittsburgh, PA 15213
Phone: (412) 681-1800

#338
Original Oyster House
Cuisines: Seafood
Average price: Inexpensive
Area: Downtown
Address: 20 Market Sq
Pittsburgh, PA 15222
Phone: (412) 566-7925

#339
Pallantia Tapas de España
Cuisines: Spanish, Tapas Bar, Cocktail Bar
Average price: Modest
Area: Shadyside
Address: 810 Ivy St
Pittsburgh, PA 15232
Phone: (412) 621-2919

#340
Wai Wai Chinese Cuisine
Cuisines: Chinese
Average price: Inexpensive
Area: Bloomfield
Address: 4717 Liberty Ave
Pittsburgh, PA 15224
Phone: (412) 621-0133

#341
The Livermore
Cuisines: Tapas/Small Plates
Average price: Modest
Area: East Liberty
Address: 124 S Highland Ave
Pittsburgh, PA 15206
Phone: (412) 361-0600

#342
Peppi's
Cuisines: Sandwiches
Average price: Inexpensive
Area: Downtown
Address: 12 Smithfield St
Pittsburgh, PA 15222
Phone: (412) 281-1510

#343
Alexander's Italian Bistro
Cuisines: Italian
Average price: Modest
Area: Bloomfield
Address: 5104 Liberty Ave
Pittsburgh, PA 15224
Phone: (412) 357-8197

#344
SLICE on Broadway
Cuisines: Pizza
Average price: Inexpensive
Area: Beechview
Address: 2128 Broadway Ave
Pittsburgh, PA 15216
Phone: (412) 531-1068

#345
Heinz USA
Cuisines: Cafe
Average price: Inexpensive
Area: Troy Hill
Address: 1062 Progress St
Pittsburgh, PA 15212
Phone: (412) 237-5757

#346
Korea Garden
Cuisines: Korean
Average price: Modest
Area: Oakland
Address: 414 Semple St
Pittsburgh, PA 15213
Phone: (412) 681-6460

#347
Cornerstone Restaurant & Bar
Cuisines: American, Breakfast & Brunch
Average price: Modest
Area: Aspinwall
Address: 301 Freeport Rd
Pittsburgh, PA 15215
Phone: (412) 408-3420

#348
The Melting Pot
Cuisines: Fondue
Average price: Expensive
Area: South Side
Address: 125 W Station Square Dr
Pittsburgh, PA 15219
Phone: (412) 261-3477

#349
Frank & Shirley's Restaurant
Cuisines: American, Diner
Average price: Inexpensive
Area: Overbrook
Address: 2209 Saw Mill Run Blvd
Pittsburgh, PA 15210
Phone: (412) 882-3550

#350
Groceria Italiana
Cuisines: Grocery, Deli
Average price: Inexpensive
Area: Bloomfield
Address: 237 Cedarville St
Pittsburgh, PA 15224
Phone: (412) 681-1227

#351
Little Tokyo Bistro
Cuisines: Sushi Bar, Japanese, Korean
Average price: Modest
Area: South Side
Address: 2122 E Carson St
Pittsburgh, PA 15203
Phone: (412) 488-9986

#352
Jozsa Corner
Cuisines: Hungarian
Average price: Modest
Area: Hazelwood
Address: 4800 2nd Ave
Pittsburgh, PA 15207
Phone: (412) 422-1886

#353
Poros
Cuisines: Mediterranean, Greek, Seafood
Average price: Modest
Area: Downtown
Address: 2 PPG Pl
Pittsburgh, PA 15222
Phone: (412) 904-2051

#354
Vietnam's Pho
Cuisines: Vietnamese
Average price: Inexpensive
Area: Strip District
Address: 1627 Penn Ave
Pittsburgh, PA 15222
Phone: (412) 281-8881

#355
Texas de Brazil
Cuisines: Brazilian, Steakhouse
Average price: Expensive
Area: South Side
Address: 240 W Station Square Dr
Pittsburgh, PA 15219
Phone: (412) 230-4004

#356
O'Leary's
Cuisines: Diner
Average price: Inexpensive
Area: South Side
Address: 1412 E Carson St
Pittsburgh, PA 15289
Phone: (412) 431-8100

#357
Barb's Corner Kitchen
Cuisines: Breakfast & Brunch, Diner
Average price: Inexpensive
Area: Lawrenceville
Address: 4711 Butler St
Pittsburgh, PA 15201
Phone: (412) 621-2644

#358
Curry on Murray
Cuisines: Thai
Average price: Modest
Area: Squirrel Hill
Address: 2121 Murray Ave
Pittsburgh, PA 15217
Phone: (412) 422-3120

#359
Redbeard's On Sixth
Cuisines: American, Sports Bar
Average price: Modest
Area: Downtown
Address: 144 6th St
Pittsburgh, PA 15222
Phone: (412) 261-2324

#360
Silk Elephant
Cuisines: Thai, Tapas Bar
Average price: Modest
Area: Squirrel Hill
Address: 1712 Murray Ave
Pittsburgh, PA 15217
Phone: (412) 421-8801

Pittsburgh Restaurant Guide 2018 / Restaurants, Bars & Cafés

#361
Hambone's Neighborhood Bar and Grill
Cuisines: Pub, American
Average price: Inexpensive
Area: Lawrenceville
Address: 4207 Butler St
Pittsburgh, PA 15201
Phone: (412) 681-4318

#362
The Alcove
Cuisines: Sandwiches, Diner, Deli
Average price: Inexpensive
Area: Greentree
Address: 875 Greentree Rd
Pittsburgh, PA 15220
Phone: (412) 458-0075

#363
Vincent's of Greentree
Cuisines: Pizza, Italian
Average price: Modest
Area: Greentree
Address: 333 Mansfield Ave
Pittsburgh, PA 15220
Phone: (412) 921-8811

#364
The Elbow Room
Cuisines: American, Burgers, Sandwiches
Average price: Modest
Area: Shadyside
Address: 5744 1/2 Ellsworth Ave
Pittsburgh, PA 15232
Phone: (412) 441-5222

#365
Hemingway's Cafe
Cuisines: Dive Bar, American
Average price: Inexpensive
Area: Oakland
Address: 3911 Forbes Ave
Pittsburgh, PA 15213
Phone: (412) 621-4100

#366
Lulu's Noodles
Cuisines: Chinese, Noodles
Average price: Inexpensive
Area: Oakland
Address: 400 S Craig St
Pittsburgh, PA 15213
Phone: (412) 687-7777

#367
Deli on Butler Street
Cuisines: Deli
Average price: Inexpensive
Area: Lawrenceville
Address: 4034 Butler St
Pittsburgh, PA 15201
Phone: (412) 682-6866

#368
V3 Flatbread Pizza
Cuisines: Pizza, Gluten-Free
Average price: Inexpensive
Area: Downtown
Address: 11 Fifth Ave
Pittsburgh, PA 15222
Phone: (412) 456-0500

#369
Mike & Tony's Gyros
Cuisines: Greek, Mediterranean
Average price: Inexpensive
Area: South Side
Address: 1414 E Carson St
Pittsburgh, PA 15203
Phone: (412) 431-2299

#370
Mama Rose
Cuisines: Caribbean
Average price: Inexpensive
Area: Larimer
Address: 121 Mayflower St
Pittsburgh, PA 15206
Phone: (412) 661-3548

#371
BD's Mongolian Grill
Cuisines: Mongolian, Asian Fusion
Average price: Modest
Area: South Side
Address: 428 S 27th St
Pittsburgh, PA 15203
Phone: (412) 390-1100

#372
Ka Mei
Cuisines: Cantonese
Average price: Modest
Area: Squirrel Hill
Address: 2209 Murray Ave
Pittsburgh, PA 15217
Phone: (412) 422-2828

#373
Bill's Bar & Burger
Cuisines: Burgers, Cocktail Bar, American
Average price: Modest
Area: Downtown
Address: 1001 Liberty Ave
Pittsburgh, PA 15222
Phone: (412) 567-2300

#374
Bloomfield Bridge Tavern
Cuisines: Dive Bar, Polish
Average price: Inexpensive
Area: Bloomfield
Address: 4412 Liberty Ave
Pittsburgh, PA 15224
Phone: (412) 682-8611

#375
Eat Unique
Cuisines: Deli
Average price: Inexpensive
Area: Oakland
Address: 305 S Craig St
Pittsburgh, PA 15213
Phone: (412) 683-9993

#376
People's Indian Restaurant
Cuisines: Indian
Average price: Modest
Area: Garfield
Address: 5147 Penn Ave
Pittsburgh, PA 15224
Phone: (412) 661-3160

#377
Lindos Restaurant
Cuisines: Greek, Breakfast & Brunch, Diner
Average price: Inexpensive
Area: North Side
Address: 947 Western Ave
Pittsburgh, PA 15233
Phone: (412) 231-0110

#378
Packs & Dogs
Cuisines: Bar, Hot Dogs
Average price: Inexpensive
Area: Mt. Washington
Address: 223 Shiloh St
Pittsburgh, PA 15211
Phone: (412) 431-1855

#379
Wings Over Pittsburgh
Cuisines: Diner, Bar
Average price: Modest
Area: South Side
Address: 2525 E Carson St
Pittsburgh, PA 15203
Phone: (412) 301-9464

#380
Nine On Nine
Cuisines: American
Average price: Expensive
Area: Downtown
Address: 900 Penn Ave
Pittsburgh, PA 15222
Phone: (412) 338-6463

#381
Beto's Pizza
Cuisines: Pizza, Salad, Sandwiches
Average price: Inexpensive
Area: Beechview, Banksville
Address: 1473 Banksville Rd
Pittsburgh, PA 15216
Phone: (412) 561-0121

#382
The Simple Greek
Cuisines: Greek
Average price: Inexpensive
Area: Downtown
Address: 431 Market St
Pittsburgh, PA 15222
Phone: (412) 261-4976

#383
S&D Cafe
Cuisines: Cafe, Sandwiches
Average price: Inexpensive
Area: The Hill District
Address: 1425 Forbes Ave
Pittsburgh, PA 15219
Phone: (412) 281-1819

#384
Sammy's Famous Corned Beef
Cuisines: Sandwiches
Average price: Inexpensive
Area: Downtown
Address: 217 9th St
Pittsburgh, PA 15222
Phone: (412) 765-2244

#385
Rasta House Caribbean Resturant
Cuisines: Caribbean
Average price: Modest
Area: North Side
Address: 1204 Federal St
Pittsburgh, PA 15212
Phone: (412) 321-2055

#386
Thai Me Up
Cuisines: Thai
Average price: Modest
Area: South Side
Address: 118 S 23rd St
Pittsburgh, PA 15203
Phone: (412) 488-8893

#387
Smallman Street Deli
Cuisines: Deli
Average price: Inexpensive
Area: Strip District
Address: 2840 Smallman St
Pittsburgh, PA 15222
Phone: (412) 434-5800

#388
Mekong Restaurant
Cuisines: Vietnamese, Chinese, Asian Fusion
Average price: Modest
Area: Dormont
Address: 1429 Potomac Ave
Pittsburgh, PA 15216
Phone: (412) 531-8066

#389
The Cheesecake Factory
Cuisines: Desserts, American
Average price: Modest
Area: South Side
Address: 415 S 27th St
Pittsburgh, PA 15203
Phone: (412) 431-7800

#390
Restaurant Hana
Cuisines: Sushi Bar
Average price: Modest
Area: Lawrenceville
Address: 4407 Butler St
Pittsburgh, PA 15201
Phone: (412) 235-7555

#391
Excuses Bar & Grill
Cuisines: Bar, American
Average price: Inexpensive
Area: South Side
Address: 2526 E Carson St
Pittsburgh, PA 15203
Phone: (412) 431-4090

#392
Tonic Bar & Grill
Cuisines: American, Cocktail Bar
Average price: Modest
Area: Downtown
Address: 971 Liberty Ave
Pittsburgh, PA 15222
Phone: (412) 456-0460

#393
Tazza D'oro Cafe & Espresso Bar
Cuisines: Coffee & Tea, Cafe
Average price: Inexpensive
Area: Highland Park
Address: 1125 N Highland Ave
Pittsburgh, PA 15206
Phone: (412) 362-3676

#394
Bartram House Bakery & Cafe
Cuisines: Cafe, Bakery, Desserts
Average price: Modest
Area: South Side
Address: 2612 E Carson St
Pittsburgh, PA 15203
Phone: (412) 235-9437

#395
Osteria 2350
Cuisines: Italian
Average price: Modest
Area: Strip District
Address: 2350 Railroad St
Pittsburgh, PA 15222
Phone: (412) 281-6595

#396
Orient Kitchen
Cuisines: Chinese
Average price: Modest
Area: Bloomfield
Address: 4808 Baum Blvd
Pittsburgh, PA 15213
Phone: (412) 682-3311

#397
Chinatown Inn
Cuisines: Chinese
Average price: Modest
Area: Downtown
Address: 520 3rd Ave
Pittsburgh, PA 15219
Phone: (412) 261-1292

#398
Gandy Dancer Saloon
Cuisines: Bar, Seafood, Sandwiches
Average price: Expensive
Area: South Side
Address: 100 W Station Sq Dr
Pittsburgh, PA 15219
Phone: (412) 261-1717

#399
Gaby Et Jules
Cuisines: Bakery, French, Macarons
Average price: Modest
Area: Squirrel Hill
Address: 5837 Forbes Ave
Pittsburgh, PA 15217
Phone: (412) 682-1966

#400
Emilliano's Mexican Restaurant and Bar
Cuisines: Mexican, Bar
Average price: Modest
Area: South Side
Address: 2557 E Carson St
Pittsburgh, PA 15203
Phone: (412) 381-2229

#401
That's Amore
Cuisines: Pizza
Average price: Modest
Area: Lawrenceville
Address: 5123 Butler St
Pittsburgh, PA 15201
Phone: (412) 782-9922

#402
I Tea Cafe
Cuisines: Taiwanese, Bubble Tea
Average price: Modest
Area: Shadyside
Address: 709 Bellefonte St
Pittsburgh, PA 15232
Phone: (412) 688-8330

#403
Franktuary
Cuisines: Hot Dogs, Salad
Average price: Inexpensive
Area: Downtown
Address: 115 Forbes Ave
Pittsburgh, PA 15222
Phone: (412) 281-0115

#404
Bella Vista
Cuisines: Italian
Average price: Expensive
Area: Duquesne Heights
Address: 1204 Grandview Ave
Pittsburgh, PA 15211
Phone: (412) 431-1660

#405
Smallman Street Deli
Cuisines: Deli
Average price: Modest
Area: Squirrel Hill
Address: 1912 Murray Ave
Pittsburgh, PA 15217
Phone: (412) 421-3354

#406
Asiatique Thai Bistro
Cuisines: Thai
Average price: Modest
Area: Shadyside
Address: 6525 Penn Ave
Pittsburgh, PA 15206
Phone: (412) 441-1212

#407
August Henry's City Saloon
Cuisines: American
Average price: Modest
Area: Downtown
Address: 946 Penn Ave
Pittsburgh, PA 15222
Phone: (412) 765-3270

#408
Elevation Restaurant
Cuisines: American, Comfort Food
Average price: Modest
Area: Downtown
Address: 535 Smithfield St.
Pittsburgh, PA 15222
Phone: (412) 338-2200

#409
Patron Mexican Grill
Cuisines: Mexican
Average price: Modest
Area: East Liberty
Address: 133 S Highland Ave
Pittsburgh, PA 15206
Phone: (412) 441-2111

#410
Love Yogurt
Cuisines: Desserts, Ice Cream, Ramen
Average price: Inexpensive
Area: Oakland
Address: 229 Atwood St
Pittsburgh, PA 15213
Phone: (412) 381-6668

#411
Gus' Cafe
Cuisines: American, Dive Bar, Mexican
Average price: Inexpensive
Area: Lawrenceville
Address: 4717 Butler St
Pittsburgh, PA 15201
Phone: (412) 315-7271

#412
Joe's Crab Shack
Cuisines: Seafood
Average price: Modest
Area: South Side
Address: 226 W Station Square Dr
Pittsburgh, PA 15219
Phone: (412) 690-2404

#413
Mullaneys Harp and Fiddle
Cuisines: Irish, Pub
Average price: Modest
Area: Strip District
Address: 2329 Penn Ave
Pittsburgh, PA 15222
Phone: (412) 642-6622

#414
Buon Giorno Cafe
Cuisines: Italian, European, Cafe
Average price: Modest
Area: Downtown
Address: 6 Smithfield St
Pittsburgh, PA 15222
Phone: (412) 471-9048

#415
Food Shoppe
Cuisines: Grocery, Sandwiches, Deli
Average price: Inexpensive
Area: Squirrel Hill
Address: 5878 Northumberland St
Pittsburgh, PA 15217
Phone: (412) 521-0718

#416
Sciulli's Pizza
Cuisines: Pizza
Average price: Inexpensive
Area: Oakland
Address: 3404 5th Ave
Pittsburgh, PA 15213
Phone: (412) 687-9287

#417
Eggs-R-Us
Cuisines: Breakfast & Brunch
Average price: Inexpensive
Area: West End
Address: 2350 Noblestown Rd
Pittsburgh, PA 15205
Phone: (412) 922-5828

#418
Roland's Seafood Grill
Cuisines: Seafood
Average price: Modest
Area: Strip District
Address: 1904 Penn Ave
Pittsburgh, PA 15222
Phone: (412) 261-3401

#419
Bangkok Balcony
Cuisines: Thai
Average price: Modest
Area: Squirrel Hill
Address: 5846 Forbes Ave
Pittsburgh, PA 15217
Phone: (412) 521-0728

#420
Habitat Restaurant
Cuisines: American
Average price: Expensive
Area: Downtown
Address: 510 Market St
Pittsburgh, PA 15222
Phone: (412) 773-8848

#421
Gio's Cafe
Cuisines: Italian, Cafe
Average price: Inexpensive
Area: Downtown
Address: 625 Stanwix St
Pittsburgh, PA 15222
Phone: (412) 690-5160

#422
Hyde Park Prime Steakhouse
Cuisines: Steakhouse
Average price: Expensive
Area: North Side
Address: 247 N Shore Dr
Pittsburgh, PA 15212
Phone: (412) 222-4014

#423
Palmyra Mediterrean Cuisine
Cuisines: Mediterranean
Average price: Inexpensive
Area: Downtown
Address: 10 Smithfield St
Pittsburgh, PA 15222
Phone: (412) 690-2340

#424
Frankie's Extra Long
Cuisines: Sandwiches
Average price: Inexpensive
Area: Lawrenceville
Address: 3535 Butler St
Pittsburgh, PA 15201
Phone: (412) 687-5220

#425
Nakama
Cuisines: Japanese, Sushi Bar
Average price: Modest
Area: South Side
Address: 1611 E Carson St
Pittsburgh, PA 15203
Phone: (412) 381-6000

#426
Tenders Pittsburgh
Cuisines: American, Asian Fusion
Average price: Inexpensive
Area: Oakland
Address: 121 Oakland Ave
Pittsburgh, PA 15213
Phone: (412) 683-1871

#427
Lesvos Gyros
Cuisines: Greek
Average price: Inexpensive
Area: South Side
Address: 1502 E Carson St
Pittsburgh, PA 15203
Phone: (412) 431-1121

#428
Sharp Edge Beer Emporium
Cuisines: American, Belgian, Pub
Average price: Modest
Area: East Liberty
Address: 302 S St Clair St
Pittsburgh, PA 15206
Phone: (412) 661-3537

#429
Everyday's A Sundae
Cuisines: Sandwiches,
Coffee & Tea, Ice Cream
Average price: Inexpensive
Area: Shadyside
Address: 6014 Centre Ave
Pittsburgh, PA 15206
Phone: (412) 363-2233

#430
Scoglio's Greentree
Cuisines: Italian
Average price: Modest
Area: Greentree
Address: 661 Andersen Dr, Bldg 7
Pittsburgh, PA 15220
Phone: (412) 921-1062

#431
Crystal On Penn
Cuisines: Mediterranean
Average price: Modest
Area: Strip District
Address: 1211 Penn Ave
Pittsburgh, PA 15222
Phone: (412) 434-0480

#432
Cain's Saloon
Cuisines: American
Average price: Modest
Area: Dormont
Address: 3239 W Liberty Ave
Pittsburgh, PA 15216
Phone: (412) 561-7444

#433
Lin's Asian Fusion
Cuisines: Asian Fusion
Average price: Modest
Area: South Side
Address: 2018 E Carson St
Pittsburgh, PA 15203
Phone: (412) 251-0228

#434
Sorrento's Pizza
Cuisines: Pizza
Average price: Inexpensive
Area: Oakland
Address: 233 Atwood St
Pittsburgh, PA 15213
Phone: (412) 621-9129

#435
Aracri's Greentree Inn
Cuisines: American, Italian, Seafood
Average price: Expensive
Area: Greentree
Address: 1006 Greentree Rd
Pittsburgh, PA 15220
Phone: (412) 921-4601

#436
The Hop House
Cuisines: Bar, American, Music Venue
Average price: Modest
Area: Greentree
Address: 2749 Noblestown Rd
Pittsburgh, PA 15205
Phone: (412) 922-9560

#437
Las Velas
Cuisines: Mexican
Average price: Modest
Area: Downtown
Address: 21 Market Sq
Pittsburgh, PA 15222
Phone: (412) 251-0031

#438
Morton's The Steakhouse
Cuisines: Steakhouse
Average price: Exclusive
Area: Downtown
Address: 625 Liberty Ave
Pittsburgh, PA 15222
Phone: (412) 261-7141

#439
Riviera Pizza & Pasta
Cuisines: Pizza, Italian, Burgers
Average price: Inexpensive
Area: North Side
Address: 1213 Spring Garden Ave
Pittsburgh, PA 15212
Phone: (412) 322-1100

#440
Teutonia Mannerchor
Cuisines: German, Beer, Wine & Spirits
Average price: Modest
Area: North Side
Address: 857 Phineas St
Pittsburgh, PA 15212
Phone: (412) 231-9141

#441
Steel Cactus
Cuisines: Mexican
Average price: Modest
Area: South Side
Address: 1831 E Carson St
Pittsburgh, PA 15203
Phone: (412) 431-3535

#442
Giovanni's Pizza & Pasta
Cuisines: Pizza, Italian, Salad
Average price: Modest
Area: Downtown
Address: 123 6th St
Pittsburgh, PA 15222
Phone: (412) 281-7060

#443
Sumi's Cakery
Cuisines: Bakery, Korean, Desserts
Average price: Inexpensive
Area: Squirrel Hill
Address: 2119 Murray Ave
Pittsburgh, PA 15217
Phone: (412) 419-1038

#444
Lydiah's Coffee House
Cuisines: African, Coffee & Tea
Average price: Inexpensive
Area: Downtown
Address: 200 Grant St
Pittsburgh, PA 15219
Phone: (412) 281-4701

#445
Thai Gourmet
Cuisines: Thai
Average price: Modest
Area: Bloomfield
Address: 4505 Liberty Ave
Pittsburgh, PA 15224
Phone: (412) 681-4373

#446
Original Hot Dog Shop
Cuisines: Hot Dogs, Burgers, Pizza
Average price: Inexpensive
Area: Oakland
Address: 3901 Forbes Ave
Pittsburgh, PA 15213
Phone: (412) 621-7388

#447
Ali Baba Restaurant
Cuisines: Middle Eastern
Average price: Modest
Area: Oakland
Address: 404 S Craig St
Pittsburgh, PA 15213
Phone: (412) 682-2829

#448
Coach's Bottleshop & Grille
Cuisines: American, Burgers, Bar
Average price: Modest
Area: Banksville
Address: 3105 Banksville Rd
Pittsburgh, PA 15216
Phone: (412) 207-9397

#449
Primanti Bros.
Cuisines: Sandwiches, American, Sports Bar
Average price: Inexpensive
Area: South Side
Address: 1832 East Carson St
Pittsburgh, PA 15203
Phone: (412) 381-2583

#450
Mendoza Express
Cuisines: Mexican
Average price: Inexpensive
Area: East Carnegie, Greentree
Address: 812 Noblestown Rd
Pittsburgh, PA 15205
Phone: (412) 429-8780

#451
Amazing Wok
Cuisines: Chinese
Average price: Inexpensive
Area: Dormont
Address: 2910 W Liberty Ave
Pittsburgh, PA 15216
Phone: (412) 343-8686

#452
Il Tetto: A Rooftop Beer Garden
Cuisines: Italian, Bar
Average price: Modest
Area: Downtown
Address: 942 Penn Ave
Pittsburgh, PA 15222
Phone: (412) 281-2810

#453
Mediterrano
Cuisines: Greek, Mediterranean
Average price: Modest
Area: West View
Address: 2193 Babcock Blvd
Pittsburgh, PA 15209
Phone: (412) 822-8888

#454
Sakura Teppanyaki & Sushi
Cuisines: Sushi Bar, Japanese
Average price: Modest
Area: Squirrel Hill
Address: 5882 Forbes Ave
Pittsburgh, PA 15217
Phone: (412) 422-7188

#455
Rialto Pizza
Cuisines: Pizza, Ice Cream, Desserts
Average price: Inexpensive
Area: Greenfield
Address: 623 Greenfield Ave
Pittsburgh, PA 15207
Phone: (412) 421-2121

#456
Maiku Sushi
Cuisines: Sushi Bar
Average price: Inexpensive
Area: Strip District
Address: 1611 Penn Ave
Pittsburgh, PA 15222
Phone: (412) 281-8888

#457
Culture
Cuisines: American
Average price: Modest
Area: Downtown
Address: 130 7th St
Pittsburgh, PA 15222
Phone: (412) 338-2222

#458
Slice On Broadway
Cuisines: Salad, Pizza, Sandwiches
Average price: Modest
Area: North Side
Address: 115 Federal Street
Pittsburgh, PA 15212
Phone: (412) 325-4485

#459
Pino's Contemporary Italian Restaurant & Wine Bar
Cuisines: Italian, Tapas/Small Plates
Average price: Modest
Area: Point Breeze
Address: 6738 Reynolds St
Pittsburgh, PA 15206
Phone: (412) 361-1336

#460
Aiello's Pizza
Cuisines: Pizza, Italian
Average price: Inexpensive
Area: Squirrel Hill
Address: 2112 Murray Ave
Pittsburgh, PA 15217
Phone: (412) 521-9973

#461
The Goldmark
Cuisines: Cocktail Bar, Music Venue, American
Average price: Modest
Area: Lawrenceville
Address: 4517 Butler St
Pittsburgh, PA 15201
Phone: (412) 688-8820

#462
Pittsburgh Fish & Chicken
Cuisines: Fish & Chips, Chicken Wings, Seafood
Average price: Modest
Area: Brighton Heights
Address: 1312 Benton Ave
Pittsburgh, PA 15212
Phone: (412) 761-0776

#463
The Carlton
Cuisines: American
Average price: Expensive
Area: Downtown
Address: 500 Grant St
Pittsburgh, PA 15219
Phone: (412) 391-4099

#464
Cherries Diner
Cuisines: Diner, Breakfast & Brunch
Average price: Inexpensive
Area: Downtown
Address: 212 Forbes Ave
Pittsburgh, PA 15222
Phone: (412) 281-8182

#465
Pizza Italia
Cuisines: Pizza
Average price: Modest
Area: Bloomfield
Address: 4512 Liberty Ave
Pittsburgh, PA 15224
Phone: (412) 621-8960

#466
Forbes Gyro
Cuisines: Middle Eastern, Turkish, Pizza
Average price: Inexpensive
Area: Oakland
Address: 3715 Forbes Ave
Pittsburgh, PA 15213
Phone: (412) 621-2140

#467
Tom's Diner
Cuisines: Greek, Burgers, Sandwiches
Average price: Inexpensive
Area: Dormont
Address: 2937 W Liberty Ave
Pittsburgh, PA 15216
Phone: (412) 531-2350

#468
Noodles & Company
Cuisines: Noodles
Average price: Modest
Area: Downtown
Address: 476 McMaster Way
Pittsburgh, PA 15222
Phone: (412) 562-2191

#469
New Dumpling House
Cuisines: Chinese, Asian Fusion
Average price: Modest
Area: Squirrel Hill
Address: 2138 Murray Ave
Pittsburgh, PA 15217
Phone: (412) 422-4178

#470
Senti
Cuisines: Italian, Wine Bar
Average price: Modest
Area: Lawrenceville
Address: 3473 Butler St
Pittsburgh, PA 15201
Phone: (412) 586-4347

#471
American Natural
Cuisines: Convenience Store, Sandwiches
Average price: Modest
Area: South Side
Address: 73 E Carson St
Pittsburgh, PA 15219
Phone: (412) 471-1529

#472
Mineo's Pizza House
Cuisines: Pizza
Average price: Inexpensive
Area: Squirrel Hill
Address: 2128 Murray Ave
Pittsburgh, PA 15217
Phone: (412) 521-2053

#473
Alex's Corner Pizza Shop
Cuisines: Pizza
Average price: Inexpensive
Area: Bloomfield
Address: 4902 Cypress St
Pittsburgh, PA 15224
Phone: (412) 683-2817

#474
Claddagh Irish Pub
Cuisines: Pub, Irish
Average price: Modest
Area: South Side
Address: 407 Cinema Dr
Pittsburgh, PA 15203
Phone: (412) 381-4800

#475
Wiggy's
Cuisines: Chicken Wings
Average price: Inexpensive
Area: West End
Address: 2350 Noblestown Rd
Pittsburgh, PA 15205
Phone: (412) 919-0361

#476
Charya's
Cuisines: Steakhouse, Seafood, Italian
Average price: Modest
Area: Bethel Park
Address: 2973 S Park Rd
Bethel Park, PA 15102
Phone: (412) 567-5123

#477
Taste of India
Cuisines: Indian
Average price: Modest
Area: Bloomfield
Address: 4320 Penn Ave
Pittsburgh, PA 15224
Phone: (412) 681-7700

#478
Paisano's
Cuisines: Pizza
Average price: Inexpensive
Area: Allentown
Address: 821 E Warrington Ave
Pittsburgh, PA 15210
Phone: (412) 381-5530

#479
Mike & Tony's Gyros
Cuisines: Greek, Mediterranean
Average price: Inexpensive
Area: Downtown
Address: 927 Liberty Ave
Pittsburgh, PA 15222
Phone: (412) 391-4077

#480
Milky Way
Cuisines: Pizza, Kosher
Average price: Inexpensive
Area: Squirrel Hill
Address: 2120 Murray Ave
Pittsburgh, PA 15217
Phone: (412) 421-3121

Pittsburgh Restaurant Guide 2018 / Restaurants, Bars & Cafés

#481
Cafe Milano
Cuisines: Pizza, Italian
Average price: Modest
Area: Downtown
Address: 134 6th St
Pittsburgh, PA 15222
Phone: (412) 281-3131

#482
Lucca
Cuisines: Italian, Seafood
Average price: Expensive
Area: Oakland
Address: 317 S Craig St
Pittsburgh, PA 15213
Phone: (412) 682-3310

#483
Andy's Sushi Bar
Cuisines: Sushi Bar
Average price: Modest
Area: Strip District
Address: 1711 Penn Ave
Pittsburgh, PA 15222
Phone: (412) 281-8272

#484
The Pita Pit
Cuisines: Sandwiches
Average price: Inexpensive
Area: South Side
Address: 2763 E Carson St
Pittsburgh, PA 15203
Phone: (412) 481-7482

#485
Chaz & Odette
Cuisines: Gluten-Free, American, Tapas Bar
Average price: Modest
Area: Bloomfield, Shadyside
Address: 5102 Baum Blvd
Pittsburgh, PA 15224
Phone: (412) 683-8300

#486
Sabroso Mexican Delights
Cuisines: Street Vendor, Mexican, Latin American
Average price: Inexpensive
Area: Strip District
Address: 1933 Penn Ave
Pittsburgh, PA 15222
Phone: (724) 234-5710

#487
East End Food Co-Op
Cuisines: Health Market, Vegetarian
Average price: Modest
Area: Point Breeze
Address: 7516 Meade St
Pittsburgh, PA 15208
Phone: (412) 242-3598

#488
Old Town Buffet
Cuisines: Buffet, Chinese
Average price: Modest
Area: Bon Air
Address: 860 Saw Mill Run Blvd
Pittsburgh, PA 15226
Phone: (412) 481-1118

#489
Szechuan Express
Cuisines: Szechuan
Average price: Inexpensive
Area: Oakland
Address: 125 Oakland Ave
Pittsburgh, PA 15213
Phone: (412) 687-8000

#490
Maietta Restaurant
Cuisines: Cafe
Average price: Inexpensive
Area: Mt. Oliver
Address: 203 Brownsville Rd
Pittsburgh, PA 15210
Phone: (412) 381-3331

#491
Angelo's Pizzeria
Cuisines: Pizza
Average price: Inexpensive
Area: Bloomfield
Address: 4766 Liberty Ave
Pittsburgh, PA 15224
Phone: (412) 621-5330

#492
The Inn on Negley
Cuisines: Bed & Breakfast, Tea Room
Average price: Expensive
Area: Shadyside
Address: 703 S Negley Ave
Pittsburgh, PA 15232
Phone: (412) 661-0631

#493
DiBella's Subs
Cuisines: Sandwiches, Salad, Deli
Average price: Inexpensive
Area: Downtown
Address: 16 Market Sq
Pittsburgh, PA 15222
Phone: (412) 338-8634

#494
Genoa Pizza & Bar
Cuisines: Pizza, Italian
Average price: Modest
Area: Downtown
Address: 111 Market St
Pittsburgh, PA 15222
Phone: (412) 281-6100

#495
Easy Street
Cuisines: American
Average price: Modest
Area: Downtown
Address: 301 Grant St
Pittsburgh, PA 15219
Phone: (412) 235-7984

#496
Beehive Coffee
Cuisines: Coffee & Tea,
Breakfast & Brunch, Vegetarian
Average price: Inexpensive
Area: South Side
Address: 1327 E Carson St
Pittsburgh, PA 15203
Phone: (412) 488-4483

#497
Hanlon's Cafe
Cuisines: American
Average price: Inexpensive
Area: Downtown
Address: 961 Liberty Ave
Pittsburgh, PA 15222
Phone: (412) 394-3500

#498
Zeke's Coffee
Cuisines: Cafe, Coffee & Tea
Average price: Inexpensive
Area: East Liberty
Address: 6015 Penn Ave
Pittsburgh, PA 15206
Phone: (412) 737-0862

#499
Peppi's
Cuisines: Sandwiches
Average price: Inexpensive
Area: Point Breeze
Address: 7619 1/2 Penn Ave
Pittsburgh, PA 15221
Phone: (412) 243-1610

#500
Redbeard's Bar & Grill
Cuisines: American, Burgers, Sports Bar
Average price: Modest
Area: Mt. Washington
Address: 201 Shiloh St
Pittsburgh, PA 15211
Phone: (412) 431-3730

Made in the USA
Columbia, SC
20 October 2020